ISBN: 9781314614275

Published by:
HardPress Publishing
8345 NW 66TH ST #2561
MIAMI FL 33166-2626

Email: info@hardpress.net
Web: http://www.hardpress.net

Date Due

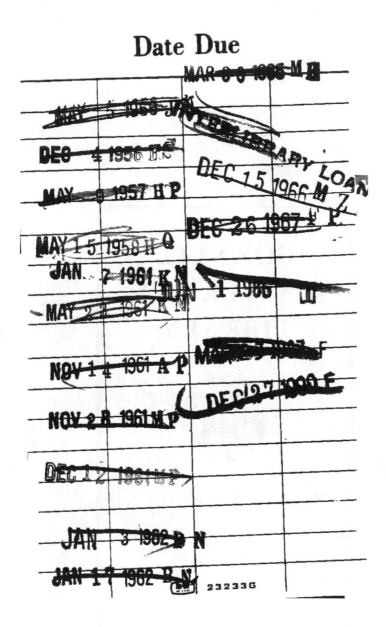

MAR 3 0 1966 M B

MAY 1 1956 J

DEC 4 1956 B C

MAY 9 1957 H P

INTER-LIBRARY LOAN

DEC 15 1966 M L

DEC 26 1967 ½ K

MAY 15 1958 H Q

JAN 7 1961 K N

JUN 1 1966 U

MAY 2 1961 R N

NOV 14 1961 A P

MAR 1961 F

NOV 2 8 1961 M P

DEC 27 1969 E

DEC 12 1961 M P

JAN 3 1962 B N

JAN 17 1962 R N

232336

THE PHILOSOPHY OF LOYALTY

BY

JOSIAH ROYCE

PROFESSOR OF THE HISTORY OF PHILOSOPHY
IN HARVARD UNIVERSITY

New York
THE MACMILLAN COMPANY
1908

G.S. 4809

COPYRIGHT, 1908,

BY THE MACMILLAN COMPANY.

Set up and electrotyped.   Published March, 1908.

Norwood Press
J. S. Cushing Co. — Berwick & Smith Co.
Norwood, Mass., U.S.A.

PREFACE

In 1906 and 1907 I gave, as a part of my regular work at the Summer School of Harvard University, an "Introduction to Ethics, with Special Reference to the Interests of Teachers." A few lectures, summing up the main principles that lay at the basis of this ethical course as it had been given in the summer of 1906, were delivered in January and February, 1907, before a general academic audience, during a brief visit of mine at the University of Illinois. In several other places, both in the West and in the East, I have also presented portions of my views upon ethics; and in the summer of 1907 four general lectures on the topic were repeated before the Summer School of Theology at Harvard. In November and December of 1907 the lectures that constitute the present book were delivered for the first time before the Lowell Institute in Boston.

In preparing this new statement of my case for the Lowell Institute course, I thus had the opportunity to use the experience and the criticisms that had resulted from several previous efforts of mine to set forth my views about the topics treated in this "Philosophy of Loyalty." The Lowell Institute lectures were, in fact, substantially a fresh presentation of the material, — only Lecture V, on "American Problems," retaining any large portion of the text of any of my former lectures. But, as the reader may see from the foregoing statement, the general doctrine contained in "The Philosophy of Loyalty" here worked out has been discussed, in various forms, and with a good many friends, pupils, and critics. I hope, therefore, that this book bears marks of the aid that I have gained from such contact with many sorts of minds, in widely different places.

During the present academic year, 1907–1908, the doctrine here presented has also been put into the form of a regular college course, which I have been permitted, as visiting lecturer, to give to undergraduate students at Yale University in weekly class-meetings.

The present book, although in this way related to present and past academic tasks, is, nevertheless, not a text-book, and does not mean to be an elaborately technical philosophical research. It is simply an appeal to any reader who may be fond of ideals, and who may also be willing to review his own ideals in a somewhat new light and in a philosophical spirit. Loyalty is indeed an old word, and to my mind a precious one; and the general idea of loyalty is still far older than the word, and is immeasurably more precious. But this idea has nearly always been confused in men's minds by its chance social and traditional associations. Everybody has heard of loyalty; most prize it; but few perceive it to be what, in its inmost spirit, it really is, — the heart of all the virtues, the central duty amongst all duties. In order to be able to see that this is the true meaning of the idea of loyalty, one has to free this idea from its unessential if somewhat settled associations with this or that special social habit or circumstance. And in order to accomplish this latter end, one has indeed to give to the term a more exact meaning than popular usage defines.

It is this freeing of the idea of loyalty from its chance and misleading associations; it is this vindication of the spirit of loyalty as the central spirit of the moral and reasonable life of man, — it is this that I believe to be somewhat new about my " Philosophy of Loyalty." The conception of " Loyalty to Loyalty," as set forth in my third lecture, constitutes the most significant part of this ethical task. For the rest, if my philosophy is, as a theory, more or less new, I am still only trying to make articulate what I believe to be the true spirit and meaning of all the loyal, whoever they may be, and however they define their fidelity.

The result of conceiving duty in terms of the conception of loyalty which is here expounded is, indeed, if I am right, somewhat deep-going and transforming, not only for ethics, but for most men's views of truth and reality, and of religion. My own general philosophical opinions have been set forth in various works some time since (most elaborately in the volumes entitled " The World and the Individual "). I have no change to report in my fundamental metaphysical theses. But I have not published any formulation of my ethical opinions since the brief review of ethical problems in the first part of my " Religious Aspect of Philosophy " (published in 1885). One learns a good deal about ethics as one matures. And I believe that this present statement of mine ought to help at least some readers to see that such philosophical idealism as I have long maintained is not a doctrine remote from life, but is in close touch with the most practical issues; and that religion, as well as daily life, has much to gain from the right union of ethics with a philosophical theory of the real world.

At the moment there is much speech, in current philosophical literature, regarding the " nature of truth " and regarding " pragmatism." An ethical treatise very naturally takes advantage of this situation to discuss the relation between the "practical" and — the Eternal. I have done so in my closing lectures. In order to do so, I have had to engage in a certain polemic regarding the problem of truth, — a polemic directed against certain opinions recently set forth by one of the dearest of my friends, and by one of the most loyal of men; my teacher for a while in my youth; my honored colleague for many years, — Professor William James. Such a polemic would be indeed much out of place in a book upon Loyalty, were it not that my friend and myself fully agree that, to both of us, truth indeed " is the greater friend." Had I not very early in my work as a student known Professor James, I doubt whether any poor book of mine would ever have been written, — least of all the present one. What I personally owe him, then, I most heartily and affectionately acknowledge. But if he and I do not see truth in the same light at present, we still do well, I think, as friends, each to speak his mind as we walk by the way, and then to wait until some other light shines for our eyes. I suppose that so to do is loyalty.

Meanwhile, I am writing, in this book, not merely and not mainly for philosophers, but for all those who love, as I said, ideals, and also for those who love, as I may now add, their country, — a country so ripe at present for idealism, and so confused, nevertheless, by the vastness and the complication of its social and political problems. To simplify men's moral issues, to clear their vision for the sight of the eternal, to win hearts for loyalty, — this would be, in this land, a peculiarly precious mission, if indeed I could hope that this book could aid, however little, towards such an end.

Amongst the numerous friends to whom (whether or no they agree with all my views) I am especially indebted for direct and indirect aid in preparing this book, and for criticisms and other suggestions, I must mention: first, my wife, who has constantly helped me with her counsel, and in the revision of my text; then, my sister, Miss Ruth Royce, of San José, California, with whom I discussed the plan of the work in the summer of 1907; then, Doctor and Mrs. R. C. Cabot of Boston; Doctor J. J. Putnam of Boston; and, finally, my honored colleague, Professor George H. Palmer.

HARVARD UNIVERSITY,
CAMBRIDGE, MASSACHUSETTS,
March 1, 1908.

CONTENTS

I

NATURE AND NEED OF LOYALTY

LECTURE I

THE NATURE AND THE NEED OF LOYALTY

ONE of the most familiar traits of our time is the tendency to revise tradition, to reconsider the foundations of old beliefs, and sometimes mercilessly to destroy what once seemed indispensable. This disposition, as we all know, is especially prominent in the realms of social theory and of religious belief. But even the exact sciences do not escape from the influence of those who are fond of the reëxamination of dogmas. And the modern tendency in question has, of late years, been very notable in the field of Ethics. Conventional morality has been required, in company with religion, and also in company with exact science, to endure the fire of criticism. And although, in all ages, the moral law has indeed been exposed to the assaults of the wayward, the peculiar moral situation of our time is this, that it is no longer either the flippant or the vicious who are the most pronounced or the most dangerous opponents of our moral traditions. Devoted reformers, earnest public servants, ardent prophets of a coming spiritual order, — all these types of lovers of humanity are represented amongst those who to-day demand great and deep changes in the moral standards by which our lives are to be governed. We have become accustomed, during the past few generations, — during the period of Socialism and of Individualism, of Karl Marx, of Henry George, of Ibsen, of Nietzsche, of Tolstoi, — to hear unquestionably sincere lovers of humanity sometimes declaring our traditions regarding the rights of property to be immoral, and sometimes assailing, in the name of virtue, our present family ties as essentially unworthy of the highest ideals. Individualism itself, in many rebellious forms, we often find asserting that it speaks in the name of the true morality of the future. And the movement begun in Germany by Nietzsche — the tendency towards what that philosophical rhapsodist

4

called the "transmutation of all moral values" — has in recent years made popular the thesis that all the conventional morality of the past, whatever may have been its inevitableness, or its temporary usefulness, was in principle false, was a mere transition stage of evolution. and must be altered to the core. "Time makes ancient good uncouth": in this well-known word one might sum up the spirit of this modern revolt against moral traditions.

Now when we review the recent moral controversies that express this sort of questioning, some of us find ourselves especially troubled and bewildered. We all feel that if the foundations of the exact sciences are to be criticised by the restless spirit of our reforming age, the exact sciences are indeed well able to take care of themselves. And as for religion, — if its fortunes have indeed, of late, deeply troubled and perplexed many gentle hearts, still both believers and doubters have now generally come to view with a certain resignation this aspect of the fate of our time, whether they regard religious doubt as the result of God's way of dealing with a way-ward world, or as a sign of man's transition to a higher stage of enlightenment.

But restlessness regarding the very foundations of morality — that seems to many of us especially discouraging. For that concerns both the seen and the unseen world, both the truths that justify the toil spent upon exact science, and the hopes for the love of which the religions of men have seemed dear. For what is science worth, and what is religion worth, if human life itself, for whose ennoblement science and religion have both labored, has no genuine moral standards by which one may measure its value? If, then, our moral standards themselves are questioned, the iron of doubt — so some of us feel — seems to enter our very hearts.

I

In view, then, of the fact that the modern tendency to revise traditions has inevitably extended itself, in new ways, to the region of morals, I suppose that a study of some of the foundations of the moral life is a timely undertaking. It is such an undertaking that I propose as the task of the present course of lectures. My purpose, in these discussions, is both a philosophical and a practical purpose. I should indeed be glad, if there were time, to attempt, in your company, a systematic review of all the main problems of philosophical ethics. That is, I should like, were that possible, to discuss with you at length the nature, the foundation, and the truth of the moral law, approaching that problem from all those various sides which interest philosophers. And, as a fact, I shall indeed venture to say something, in the course of these lectures, regarding each of these topics. But I well know that there is no space, in eight lectures, for any adequate treatment of that branch of philosophy which is called Ethics. Nor do you come here merely or mainly for the sake of hearing what a student of philosophy chances to think about the problems of his own calling. Accordingly, I shall not try, in this place, to state to you any system of moral philosophy. Rather is it the other aspect of my purpose in appealing to you — the practical aspect, which I must especially try to bear in mind throughout these lectures.

Our age, as I have said, is a good deal perplexed regarding its moral ideals and its standards of duty. It has doubts about what is really the best plan of human life. This perplexity is not wholly due to any peculiar waywardness of our time, or to any general lack of moral seriousness. It is just our moral leaders, our reformers, our prophets, who most perplex us. Whether these revolutionary moral teachers are right or wrong, they beset us, they give us no rest, they call in doubt our moral judgments, they undertake to "transmute values." And the result, for many of us, is a practical result. It tends to deprive us of that confidence which we all need in order to be ready to do good works. It threatens to paralyze the effectiveness of many conscientious people. Hence any effort to reason calmly and constructively about the foundations of the moral life may serve, not merely to clarify our minds, but to give vigor to our deeds. In these lectures, then, I shall ask you to think indeed about moral problems, but to think for the sake of action. I shall try to give you some fragments of a moral philosophy; but I shall try to justify the philosophy through its application to life. I do not much care whether you agree with the letter of any of my philosophical formulas; but I do want to bring to your consciousness, by means of these formulas, a certain spirit in terms of which you may henceforth be helped to interpret the life that we all in common need to live. Meanwhile, I do not want merely to refute those reformers and prophets of whose perplexing assaults upon our moral traditions I have just spoken, nor yet do I want to join myself with them in perplexing you still further. I want, as far as I can, to indicate some ways whereby we may clarify and simplify our moral situation.

I indeed agree with the view that, in many ways, our traditional moral standards ought to be revised. We need a new heaven and a new earth. We do well to set out to seek for both, however hard or doubtful may be the quest. In so far as our restlessness about moral matters — our unsettlement — implies a sense of this need, it is a good thing. To use a comparison suggested by modern Biblical criticism — our conventional morality is indeed a sort of Pentateuch, made up of many ancient documents. It has often been edited afresh. It needs critical reëxamination. I am a student of philosophy. My principal business has always been criticism. I shall propose nothing in this course which I have not tried to submit to critical standards, and to revise repeatedly.

But, on the other hand, I do not believe that unsettlement is finality. Nor to my mind is the last word of human wisdom this: that the truth is inaccessible. Nor yet is the last word of wisdom this: that the truth is merely fluent and transient. I believe in the eternal. I am in quest of the eternal. As to moral standards, in particular, I do not like that mere homesickness and spiritual estrangement, and that confusion of mind about moral ideals, which is nowadays too common. I want to know the way that leads our human practical life homewards, even if that way prove to be infinitely long. I am discontented with mere discontent. I want, as well as I can, not merely to help you to revise some of your moral standards, but to help you to give to this revision some definitive form and tendency, some image and hint of finality.

Moreover, since moral standards, as Antigone said, are not of to-day or yesterday, I believe that revision does not mean, in this field, a mere break with the past. I myself have spent my life in revising my opinions. And yet, whenever I have most carefully revised my moral standards, I am always able to see, upon reviewing my course of thought, that at best I have been finding out, in some new light, the true meaning that was latent in old traditions. Those traditions were often better in spirit than the fathers knew. We who revise may sometimes be able to see this better meaning that was latent in forms such as are now antiquated, and perhaps, in their old literal interpretation, even mischievous. Revision does not mean mere destruction. We can often say to tradition: That which thou sowest is not quickened except it die. But we can sometimes see in the world of opinion a sort of resurrection of the dead, — a resurrection wherein what was indeed justly sown in dishonor is raised in honor, — glorified, — and perhaps incorruptible. Let us bury the natural body of tradition. What we want is its glorified body and its immortal soul.

II

I have entitled these lectures, "The Philosophy of Loyalty." I may as well confess at once that my title was suggested to me, early last summer, by a book that I read — a recent work by a distinguished ethnologist, Dr. Rudolf Steinmetz of The Hague, entitled "The Philosophy of War." War and loyalty have been, in the past, two very closely associated ideas. It will be part of the task of these lectures to break up, so far as I can, in your own minds, that ancient and disastrous association, and to show how much the true conception of loyalty has been obscured by viewing the warrior as the most typical representative of rational loyalty. Steinmetz, however, accepts, in this respect, the traditional view. According to him, war gives an opportunity for loyal devotion so notable and important that, if war were altogether abolished, one of the greatest goods of civilization would thereby be hopelessly lost. I am keenly conscious of the sharp contrast between Steinmetz's theory of loyalty and my own. I agree with Steinmetz, as you will later see, regarding the significance of loyalty as a central principle of the moral life. I disagree with him very profoundly as to the relation of war both to true loyalty and to civilization in general. The very contrast has suggested to me the adoption of the form of title which Steinmetz has used.

The phrase, "Philosophy of Loyalty," is intended to indicate first, that we are here to consider loyalty as an ethical principle. For philosophy deals with first principles. And secondly, my title means to suggest that we are to view the matter critically and discriminatingly, as well as practically. For philosophy is essentially a criticism of life. Not everything, then, that calls itself loyalty, and not every form of loyalty, shall be put in our discussion on the same level with every other moral quality that uses or that deserves the ancient name in question. Moreover, the term "loyalty" comes to us as a good old popular word, without any exact definition. We are hereafter to define our term as precisely as possible, yet so as to preserve the spirit of the former usage. In estimating the place of loyalty in the moral life, we are, moreover, to follow neither traditional authority nor the voice of private prejudice. We are to use our reason as best we can; for philosophy is an effort to think out the reasons for our opinions. We are not to praise blindly, nor to condemn according to our moods. Where loyalty seems to be a good, we are to see why; when what men call loyalty leads them astray, we are to find wherein the fault lies. Since loyalty is a relative term, and always implies that there is some object, some cause, to which any given loyalty is to be shown, we must consider what are the fitting objects of loyalty. In attempting an answer to these various questions, our philosophy of loyalty must try to delve down to the roots of human conduct, the grounds for our moral standards, as far as our time permits.

But when all these efforts have been made towards a philosophical treatment of our topic, when certain discriminations between true and mistaken loyalty have been defined, when we have insisted upon the fitting objects of loyalty, and have throughout indicated our reasons for our theses, there will then stand out one great practical lesson, which I shall try to illustrate from the start, and to bring to its fruition as our lectures close. And the lesson will be this : *In loyalty, when loyalty is properly defined, is the fulfilment of the whole moral law.* You can truthfully centre your entire moral world about a rational conception of loyalty. Justice, charity, industry, wisdom, spirituality, are all definable in terms of enlightened loyalty. And, as I shall maintain, this very way of viewing the moral world — this deliberate centralization of all the duties and of all the virtues about the one conception of rational loyalty — is of great service as a means of clarifying and simplifying the tangled moral problems of our lives and of our age.

Thus, then, I state the task which our title is intended to set before us. The rest of this opening lecture must be devoted to clearing our way — and to a merely preliminary and tentative view of our topic. I must first attempt a partial and provisional definition of the term "loyalty" as I shall use that term. I wish that I could begin with a final and adequate definition; but I cannot. Why I cannot, you will see in later lectures. At the moment I shall try to direct your minds, as well as I can, merely to some of the features that are essential to my conception of loyalty.

III

Loyalty shall mean, according to this preliminary definition: *The willing and practical and thoroughgoing devotion of a person to a cause.* A man is loyal when, first, he has some *cause* to which he is loyal; when, secondly, he *willingly* and *thoroughly* devotes himself to this cause; and when, thirdly, he expresses his devotion in some *sustained and practical way*, by acting steadily in the service of his cause. Instances of loyalty are: The devotion of a patriot to his country, when this devotion leads him actually to live and perhaps to die for his country; the devotion of a martyr to his religion; the devotion of a ship's captain to the requirements of his office when, after a disaster, he works steadily for his ship and for the saving of his ship's company until the last possible service is accomplished, so that he is the last man to leave the ship, and is ready if need be to go down with his ship.

Such cases of loyalty are typical. They involve, I have said, the willingness of the loyal man to do his service. The loyal man's cause is his cause by virtue of the assent of his own will. His devotion is his own. He chooses it, or, at all events, approves it. Moreover, his devotion is a practical one. He does something. This something serves his cause. Loyalty is never mere emotion. Adoration and affection may go with loyalty, but can never alone constitute loyalty. Furthermore, the devotion of the loyal man involves a sort of restraint or submission of his natural desires to his cause. Loyalty without self-control is impossible. The loyal man serves. That is, he does not merely follow his own impulses. He looks to his cause for guidance. This cause tells him what to do, and he does it. His devotion, furthermore, is entire. He is ready to live or to die as the cause directs.

And now for a further word about the hardest part of this preliminary definition of loyalty: A loyal man, I have said, has a cause. I do not yet say that he has a good cause. He might have a bad one. I do not say, as yet, what makes a cause a good one, and worthy of loyalty. All that is to be considered hereafter. But this. I now premise: If one is loyal, he has a cause which he indeed personally values. Otherwise, how could he be devoted to it? He therefore takes interest in the cause, loves it, is well pleased with it. On the other hand, loyalty never means the mere emotion of love for your cause, and never means merely following your own pleasure, viewed *as* your private pleasure and interest. For if you are loyal, your cause is viewed by you as something outside of you. Or if, like your country, your cause includes yourself, it is still much larger than your private self. It has its own value, so you as a loyal person believe. This essential value it would keep (so you believe) even if your private interest were left out of account. Your cause you take, then, to be something objective — something that is not your private self. It does not get its value merely from your being pleased with it. You believe, on the contrary, that you love it just because of its own value, which it has by itself, even if you die. That is just why one may be ready to die for his cause. In any case, when the loyal man serves his cause, he is not seeking his own private advantage.

Moreover, the cause to which a loyal man is devoted is never something *wholly* impersonal. It concerns other men. Loyalty is social. If one is a loyal servant of a cause, one has at least possible fellow-servants. On the other hand, since a cause, in general, tends to unite the many fellow-servants in one service, it consequently seems to the loyal man to have a sort of impersonal or superpersonal quality about it. You can love an individual. But you can be loyal only to a tie that binds you and others into some sort of unity, and loyal to individuals only through the tie. The cause to which loyalty devotes itself has always this union of the personal and the seemingly superindividual about it. It binds many individuals into one service. Loyal lovers, for instance, are loyal not merely to one another as separate individuals, but to their love, to their union, which is something more than either of them, or even than both of them viewed as distinct individuals.

So much for a preliminary view of what loyalty is. Our definition is not complete.

It raises rather than solves problems about the nature of loyalty. But thus indeed we get a first notion of the general nature of loyalty.

IV

But now for a next step. Many people find that they have a need of loyalty. Loyalty is a good thing for them. If you ask, however, why loyalty may be needed by a given man, the answer may be very complex. A patriot may, in your opinion, need loyalty, first because his country needs his service, and, as you add, he actually owes this service, and so needs to do his duty, viz. to be loyal. This first way of stating a given man's need of a given loyalty, turns upon asserting that a specific cause rightly requires of a certain man a certain service. The cause, as one holds, is good and worthy. This man actually ought to serve just that cause. Hence he stands in need of loyalty, and of just this loyalty.

But in order thus to define this man's need of loyalty, you have to determine what causes are worthy of loyalty, and why this man ought to serve his own cause. To answer such questions would apparently presuppose a whole system of morals, — a system which at this stage of our argument we have not yet in sight.

But there is another, — a simpler, and, at the outset, a lower way of estimating the value of loyalty. One may, for the time, abstract from all questions as to the value of causes. Whether a man is loyal to a good cause or to a bad cause, his own personal attitude, when he is loyal, has a certain general quality. Whoever is loyal, whatever be his cause, is devoted, is active, surrenders his private self-will, controls himself, is in love with his cause, and believes in it. The loyal man is thus in a certain state of mind which has its own value for himself. To live a loyal life, whatever be one's cause, is to live in a way which is certainly free from many well-known sources of inner dissatisfaction. Thus hesitancy is often corrected by loyalty; for the cause plainly tells the loyal man what to do. Loyalty, again, tends to unify life, to give it centre, fixity, stability.

Well, these aspects of loyalty are, so far as they go, good for the loyal man. We may therefore define our need of loyalty in a certain preliminary way. We may take what is indeed a lower view of loyalty, regarding it, for the moment, in deliberate abstraction from the cause to which one is loyal. We may thus regard loyalty, for the moment, just as a personal attitude, which is good for the loyal man himself.

Now this lower view of our need of loyalty is the one to which in the rest of this lecture I want you to attend. All that I now say is preliminary. Results belong later. Let us simply abstract from the question whether a man's cause is objectively worthy of his loyalty or not. Let us ask: What does a man gain by being loyal? Suppose that some cause, outside of and also inclusive of his private self, so appeals to a man that he believes it to be worthy, and becomes heartily loyal to it. What good does he get personally out of his loyalty? In order to answer this question, even in this preliminary way, I must indeed go rather far afield, and define for you, still very tentatively, one of the best-known and hardest of the problems of our personal life.

V

What do we live for? What is our duty? What is the true ideal of life? What is the true difference between right and wrong? What is the true good which we all need? Whoever begins seriously to consider such questions as these soon observes certain great truths about the moral life which he must take into account if his enterprise is to succeed, that is, if he is ever to answer these questions.

The first truth is this: We all of us first learned about what we ought to do, about what our ideal should be, and in general about the moral law, through some authority external to our own wills. Our teachers, our parents, our playmates, society, custom, or perhaps some church, — these taught us about one or another aspect of right and wrong. The moral law came to us from without. It often seemed to us, in so far, something other than our will, something threatening or socially compelling, or externally restraining. In so far as our moral training is still incomplete, the moral law may at any moment have to assume afresh this air of an external authority merely in order to win our due attention. But if we have learned the moral law, or any part of it, and if we do not ask any longer how we first learned, or how we may still have to learn afresh our duty, but if, on the contrary, we rather ask: "What reason can I now give to myself why a given act is truly right? What reason can I give why my duty is my duty?" —then, indeed, we find that no external authority, viewed merely as external, can give one any reason why an act is truly right or wrong. Only a calm and reasonable view of what it is that I myself really will, — only this can decide such a question. My duty is simply my own will brought to my clear self-consciousness. That which I can rightly view as good for me is simply the object of my own deepest desire set plainly before my insight.

For your own will and your own desire, once fully brought to self-consciousness, furnish the only valid reason for you to know what is right and good.

This comment which I now make upon the nature of the moral law is familiar to every serious student of ethics. In one form or another this fact, that the ultimate moral authority for each of us is determined by our own rational will, is admitted even by apparently extreme partisans of authority. Socrates long ago announced the principle in question when he taught that no man is willingly base. Plato and Aristotle employed it in developing their ethical doctrines. When St. Augustine, in a familiar passage in his Confessions, regards God's will as that in which, and in which alone, our wills can find rest and peace, he indeed makes God's will the rule of life; but he also shows that the reason why each of us, if enlightened, recognizes the divine will as right, is that, in Augustine's opinion, God has so made us for himself that our own wills are by nature inwardly restless until they rest in harmony with God's will. Our restlessness, then, so long as we are out of this harmony, gives us the reason why we find it right, if we are enlightened, to surrender our self-will.

If you want to find out, then, what is right and what is good for you, bring your own will to self-consciousness. Your duty is what you yourself will to do in so far as you clearly discover who you are, and what your place in the world is. This is, indeed, a first principle of all ethical inquiry. Kant called it the Principle of the Autonomy or self-direction of the rational will of each moral being.

But now there stands beside this first principle a second principle, equally inevitable and equally important. This principle is, that I can never find out what my own will is by merely brooding over my natural desires, or by following my momentary caprices. For by nature I am a sort of meeting place of countless streams of ancestral tendency. From moment to moment, if you consider me apart from my training, I am a collection of impulses. There is no one desire that is always present to me. Left to myself alone, I can never find out what my will is.

You may interpose here the familiar thesis that there is one desire which I always have, namely, the desire to escape from pain and to get pleasure. But as soon as you try to adjust this thesis to the facts of life, it is a thesis which simplifies nothing, and which at best simply gives me back again, under new names, that chaos of conflicting passions and interests which constitutes, apart from training, my natural life. What we naturally desire is determined for us by our countless instincts and by whatever training they have received. We want to breathe, to eat, to walk, to run, to speak, to see, to hear, to love, to fight, and, amongst other things, we want to be more or less reasonable. Now, if one of these instinctive wants of ours drives us at any moment to action, we normally take pleasure in such action, in so far as it succeeds. For action in accordance with desire means relief from tension; and that is usually accompanied with pleasure. On the other hand, a thwarted activity gives us pain. But only under special circumstances does this resulting pleasure or pain of the successful or of the hindered activity come to constitute a principal object of our desire. We all do like pleasure, and we all do shun pain. But a great deal of what we desire is desired by instinct, apart from the memory or the expectation of pleasure and pain, and often counter to the warnings that pleasure and pain have given to us. It is normal to desire food because one is hungry, rather than because one loves the pleasures of the table. It is water that the thirsty man in the desert longs for, rather than pleasure, and rather than even mere relief from pain as such. For much of the pain appears to his consciousness as largely due to his longing for water. Pain, then, is indeed an evil, but it is in part secondary to thwarted desire; while, when pain appears as a brute fact of our feelings, which we indeed hate, such pain is even then only one amongst the many ills of life, only one of the many undesirable objects. The burnt child, indeed, dreads the fire;

but the climbing child, instinctively loving the ways of his remote arboreal ancestors, is little deterred by the pain of an occasional fall.

Furthermore, if I even admitted that I always desire pleasure and relief from pain, and nothing else, I should not learn from such a principle what it is that, on the whole, I am to will to do, in order to express my desire for pleasure, and in order to escape from pain. For no art is harder than the art of pleasure seeking. I can never learn that art alone by myself. And so I cannot define my own will, and hence cannot define my duty, merely in terms of pleasure and pain.

VI

So far, then, we have a rather paradoxical situation before us. Yet it is the moral situation of every one of us. If I am to know my duty, I must consult my own reasonable will. I alone can show myself why I view this or this as my duty. But on the other hand, if I merely look within myself to find what it is that I will, my own private individual nature, apart from due training, never gives me any answer to the question: What do I will? By nature I am a victim of my ancestry, a mass of world-old passions and impulses, desiring and suffering in constantly new ways as my circumstances change, and as one or another of my natural impulses comes to the front. By nature, then, apart from a specific training, I have no personal will of my own. One of the principal tasks of my life is to learn to have a will of my own. To learn your own will, — yes, to create your own will, is one of the largest of your human undertakings.

Here, then, is the paradox. I, and only I, whenever I come to my own, can morally justify to myself my own plan of life. No outer authority can ever give me the true reason for my duty. Yet I, left to myself, can never find a plan of life. I have no inborn ideal naturally present within myself. By nature I simply go on crying out in a sort of chaotic self-will, according as the momentary play of desire determines.

Whence, then, can I learn any plan of life? The moral education of any civilized person easily reminds you how this question is, in one respect, very partially, but, so far as ordinary training goes, constantly answered. One gets one's various plans of life suggested through the models that are set before each one of us by his fellows. Plans of life first come to us in connection with our endless imitative activities. These imitative processes begin in our infancy, and run on through our whole life. We learn to play, to speak, to enter into our social realm, to take part in the ways and so in the life of mankind. This imitative social activity is itself due to our instincts as social beings. But in turn the social activities are the ones that first tend to organize all of our instincts, to give unity to our passions and impulses, to transform our natural chaos of desires into some sort of order — usually, indeed, a very imperfect order. It is our social existence, then, as imitative beings, — it is this that suggests to us the sorts of plans of life which we get when we learn a calling, when we find a business in life, when we discover our place in the social world. And so our actual plans of life, namely, our callings, our more or less settled daily activities, come to us from without. We in so far learn what our own will is by first imitating the wills of others.

Yet no, — this, once more, is never the whole truth about our social situation, and is still less the whole truth about our moral situation. By ourselves alone, we have said, we can never discover in our own inner life any one plan of life that expresses our genuine will. So then, we have said, all of our plans get suggested to us by the social order in which we grow up. But on the other hand, our social training gives us a mass of varying plans of life, — plans that are not utterly chaotic, indeed, but imperfectly ordered, — mere routine, not ideal life. Moreover, social training tends not only to teach us the way of other people, but to heighten by contrast our vague natural sense of the importance of having our own way. Social training stimulates the will of the individual self, and also teaches this self customs and devices for self-expression. We never merely imitate. Conformity attracts, but also wearies us. Meanwhile, even by imitation, we often learn how to possess, and then to carry out, our own self-will. For instance, we learn speech first by imitation; but henceforth we love to hear ourselves talk; and our whole plan of life gets affected accordingly. Speech has, indeed, its origin in social conformity. Yet the tongue is an unruly member, and wags rebelliously. Teach men customs, and you equip them with weapons for expressing their own personalities. As you train the social being, you make use of his natural submissiveness. But as a result of your training he forms plans; he interprets these plans with reference to his own personal interests; he becomes aware who he is; and he may end by becoming, if not original, then at least obstreperous. And thus society is constantly engaged in training up children who may, and often do, rebel against their mother. Social conformity gives us social power. Such power brings to us a consciousness of who and what we are. Now, for the first time, we begin to have a real will of our own. And hereupon we may discover this will to be in sharp conflict with the will of society. This is what normally happens to most of us, for a time at least, in youth.

You see, so far, how the whole process upon which man's moral life depends involves this seemingly endless play of inner and outer. How shall my duty be defined? Only by my own will, whenever that will is brought to rational self-consciousness. But what is my will? By nature I know not; for by birth I am a mere eddy in the turbulent stream of inherited human passion. How, then, shall I get a will of my own? Only through social training. That indeed gives me plans, for it teaches me the settled ways of my world. Yet no, — for such training really teaches me rather the arts whereby I may express myself. It makes me clever, ambitious, often rebellious, and in so far it teaches me how to plan opposition to the social order. The circular process thus briefly indicated goes on throughout the lives of many of us. It appears in new forms at various stages of our growth. At any moment we may meet new problems of right and wrong, relating to our plans of life. We hereupon look within, at what we call our own conscience, to find out what our duty is. But, as we do so, we discover, too often, what wayward and blind guides our own hearts so far are. So we look without, in order to understand better the ways of the social world. We cannot see the inner light. Let us try the outer one. These ways of the world appeal to our imitativeness, and so we learn from the other people how we ourselves are in this case to live. Yet no, — this very learning often makes us aware of our personal contrast with other people, and so makes us self-conscious, individualistic, critical, rebellious; and again we are thrown back on ourselves for guidance. Seeing the world's way afresh, I see that it is not my way. I revive. I assert myself. My duty, I say, is my own. And so, perhaps, I go back again to my own wayward heart.

It is this sort of process which goes on, sometimes in a hopelessly circular way, when, in some complicated situation, you are morally perplexed, and after much inner brooding give up deciding by yourself and appeal to friends for advice. The advice at first pleases you, but soon may arouse your self-will more than before. You may become, as a result, more wayward and sometimes more perplexed, the longer you continue this sort of inquiry. We all know what it is to seek advice, just with the result of finding out what it is that we do not want to do.

Neither within nor without, then, do I find what seems to me a settled authority, — a settled and harmonious plan of life, — unless, indeed, one happy sort of union takes place between the inner and the outer, between my social world and myself, between my natural waywardness and the ways of my fellows.

This happy union is the one that takes place whenever my mere social conformity, my docility as an imitative creature, turns into exactly that which, in these lectures, I shall call loyalty. Let us consider what happens in such cases.

VII

Suppose a being whose social conformity has been sufficient to enable him to learn many skilful social arts, — arts of speech, of prowess in contest, of influence over other men. Suppose that these arts have at the same time awakened this man's pride, his self-confidence, his disposition to assert himself. Such a man will have in him a good deal of what you can well call social will. He will be no mere anarchist. He will have been trained into much obedience. He will be no natural enemy of society, unless, indeed, fortune has given him extraordinary opportunities to win his way without scruples. On the other hand, this man must acquire a good deal of self-will. He becomes fond of success, of mastery, of his own demands. To be sure, he can find within himself no one naturally sovereign will. He can so far find only a general determination to define some way of his own, and to have his own way. Hence the conflicts of social will and self-will are inevitable, circular, endless, so long as this is the whole story of the man's life. By merely consulting convention, on the one hand, and his disposition to be somebody, on the other hand, this man can never find any one final and consistent plan of life, nor reach any one definition of his duty.

But now suppose that there appears in this man's life some one of the greater social passions, such as patriotism well exemplifies. Let his country be in danger. Let his elemental passion for conflict hereupon fuse with his brotherly love for his own countrymen into that fascinating and blood-thirsty form of humane but furious ecstasy, which is called the war-spirit. The mood in question may or may not be justified by the passing circumstances. For that I now care not. At its best the war-spirit is no very clear or rational state of anybody's mind. But one reason why men may love this spirit is that when it comes, it seems at once to define a plan of life, — a plan which solves the conflicts of self-will and conformity. This plan has two features: (1) it is through and through a social plan, obedient to the general will of one's country, submissive; (2) it is through and through an exaltation of the self, of the inner man, who now feels glorified through his sacrifice, dignified in his self-surrender, glad to be his country's servant and martyr, — yet sure that through this very readiness for self-destruction he wins the rank of hero.

Well, if the man whose case we are supposing gets possessed by some such passion as this, he wins for the moment the consciousness of what I call loyalty. This loyalty no longer knows anything about the old circular conflicts of self-will and of conformity. The self, at such moments, looks indeed *outwards* for its plan of life. "The country needs me," it says. It looks, meanwhile, *inwards* for the inspiring justification of this plan. "Honor, the hero's crown, the soldier's death, the patriot's devotion — these," it says, "are my will. I am not giving up this will of mine. It is my pride, my glory, my self-assertion, to be ready at my country's call." And now there is no conflict of outer and inner.

How wise or how enduring or how practical such a passion may prove, I do not yet consider. What I point out is that this war-spirit, for the time at least, makes self-sacrifice seem to be self-expression, makes obedience to the country's call seem to be the proudest sort of display of one's own powers. Honor now means submission, and to obey means to have one's way. Power and service are at one. Conformity is no longer opposed to having one's own will. One has no will but that of the country.

As a mere fact of human nature, then, there are social passions which actually tend to do at once two things: (1) to intensify our self-consciousness, to make us more than ever determined to express our own will and more than ever sure of our own rights, of our own strength, of our dignity, of our power, of our value; (2) to make obvious to us that this our will has no purpose but to do the will of some fascinating social power. This social power is the cause to which we are loyal.

Loyalty, then, fixes our attention upon some one cause, bids us look without ourselves to see what this unified cause is, shows us thus some one plan of action, and then says to us, "In this cause is your life, your will, your opportunity, your fulfilment."

Thus loyalty, viewed merely as a personal attitude, solves the paradox of our ordinary existence, by showing us outside of ourselves the cause which is to be served, and inside of ourselves the will which delights to do this service, and which is not thwarted but en-riched and expressed in such service.

I have used patriotism and the war-spirit merely as a first and familiar illustration of loyalty. But now, as we shall later see, there is no necessary connection between loyalty and war; and there are many other forms of loyalty besides the patriotic forms. Loyalty has its domestic, its religious, its commercial, its professional forms, and many other forms as well. The essence of it, whatever forms it may take, is, as I conceive the matter, this: Since no man can find a plan of life by merely looking within his own chaotic nature, he has to look without, to the world of social conventions, deeds, and causes. Now, a loyal man is one who has found, and who sees, neither mere individual fellow-men to be loved or hated, nor mere conventions, nor customs, nor laws to be obeyed, but some social cause, or some system of causes, so rich, so well knit, and, to him, so fascinating, and withal so kindly in its appeal to his natural self-will, that he says to his cause: "Thy will is mine and mine is thine. In thee I do not lose but find myself, living intensely in proportion as I live for thee." If one could find such a cause, and hold it for his lifetime before his mind, clearly observing it, passionately loving it, and yet calmly understanding it, and steadily and practically serving it, he would have one plan of life, and this plan of life would be his own plan, his own will set before him, expressing all that his self-will has ever sought. Yet this plan would also be a plan of obedience, because it would mean living for the cause.

Now, in all ages of civilized life there have been people who have won in some form a consciousness of loyalty, and who have held to such a consciousness through life. Such people may or may not have been right in their choice of a cause. But at least they have exemplified through their loyalty one feature of a rational moral life. They have known what it was to have unity of purpose.

And again, the loyal have known what it was to be free from moral doubts and scruples. Their cause has been their conscience. It has told them what to do. They have listened and obeyed, not because of what they took to be blind convention, not because of a fear of external authority, not even because of what seemed to themselves any purely private and personal intuition, but because, when they have looked first outwards at their cause, and then inwards at themselves, they have found themselves worthless in their own eyes, except when viewed as active, as confidently devoted, as willing instruments of their cause. Their cause has forbidden them to doubt; it has said: "You are mine, you cannot do otherwise." And they have said to the cause: "I am, even of my own will, thine. I have no will except thy will. Take me, use me, control me, and even thereby fulfil me and exalt me." That is again the speech of the devoted patriots, soldiers, mothers, and martyrs of our race. They have had the grace of this willing, this active loyalty.

Now, people loyal in this sense have surely existed in the world, and, as you all know, the loyal still exist amongst us. And I beg you not to object to me, at this point, that such devoted people have often been loyal to very bad causes; or that different people have been loyal to causes which were in deadly war with one another, so that loyal people must often have been falsely guided. I beg you, above all, not to interpose here the objection that our modern doubters concerning moral problems simply cannot at present see to what one cause they ought to be loyal, so that just herein, just in our inability to see a fitting and central object of loyalty, lies the root of our modern moral confusion and distraction. All those possible objections are indeed perfectly fair considerations. I shall deal with them in due time; and I am just as earnestly aware of them as you can be. But just now we are getting our first glimpse of our future philosophy of loyalty. All that you can say of the defects of loyalty leaves still untouched the one great fact that, if you want to find a way of living which surmounts doubts, and centralizes your powers, it must be some such a way as all the loyal in common have trodden, since first loyalty was known amongst men. What form of loyalty is the right one, we are hereafter to see. But unless you can find some sort of loyalty, you cannot find unity and peace in your active living. You must find, then, a cause that is really worthy of the sort of devotion that the soldiers, rushing cheerfully to certain death, have felt for their clan or for their country, and that the martyrs have shown on behalf of their faith. This cause must be indeed rational, worthy, and no object of a false devotion. But once found, it must become your conscience, must tell you the truth about your duty, and must unify, as from without and from above, your motives, your special ideals, and your plans. You ought, I say, to find such a cause, if indeed there be any ought at all. And this is my first hint of our moral code.

' But you repeat, perhaps in bewilderment, your question: "Where, in our distracted modern world, in this time when cause wars with cause, and when all old moral standards are remorselessly criticised and doubted, are we to find such a cause — a cause, all-embracing, definite, rationally compelling, supreme, certain, and fit to centralize life? What cause is there that for us would rationally justify a martyr's devotion?" I reply: "A perfectly simple consideration, derived from a study of the very spirit of loyalty itself, as this spirit is manifested by all the loyal, will soon furnish to us the unmistakable answer to this question." For the moment we have won our first distant glimpse of what I mean by the general nature of loyalty, and by our common need of loyalty.

II

INDIVIDUALISM

LECTURE II

INDIVIDUALISM

IN my opening lecture I undertook to define the personal attitude which I called loyalty, and to show that, for our own individual good, we all need loyalty, and need to find causes to which we can be loyal. This was but the beginning of our philosophy of loyalty. Before I take my next step, I must ask you briefly to review the results that we have already reached.

I

By loyalty, as you remember, I mean in this preliminary view of loyalty, the willing and practical and thoroughgoing devotion of a person to a cause. By a cause that is adapted to call forth loyalty I mean, for the first, something which seems to the loyal person to be larger than his private self, and so to be, in some respect, external to his purely individual will. This cause must, in the second place, unite him with other persons by some social tie, such as a personal friendship, or his family, or the state may, in a given case, represent. The cause, therefore, to which the loyal man is devoted, is something that appears to him to be at once personal (since it concerns both himself and other people), and impersonal, or rather, if regarded from a purely human point of view, superpersonal, because it links several human selves, perhaps a vast number of selves, into some higher social unity. You cannot be loyal to a merely impersonal abstraction; and you also cannot be loyal simply to a collection of various separate persons, viewed merely as a collection. Where there is an object of loyalty, there is, then, an union of various selves into one life. This union constitutes a cause to which one may indeed be loyal, if such is his disposition. And such an union of many in one, if known to anybody for whom a person means merely a human person, appears to be something impersonal or superpersonal, just because it is more than all those separate and private personalities whom it joins. Yet it is also intensely personal, because the union is indeed an union of selves, and so not a merely artificial abstraction.

That such causes and that a thoroughgoing, willing, practical devotion to them, such as our definition of loyalty demands — that, I say, such things exist in the world, I tried at the last time to illustrate to you. My illustrations were inadequate; for it is simply impossible to show you briefly how Protean the forms of human loyalty are, and yet how similar, amidst all this endless variety of forms, the spirit of loyalty remains, whatever the causes in question may be, and whoever the loyal people are. We began, of course, with marked, traditional, and familiar illustrations. The loyal captain, steadfastly standing by his sinking ship until his last possible duty for the service to which he belongs has been accomplished; the loyal patriot, eager to devote every power to living, and, if need be, to dying for his endangered country; the loyal religious martyr, faithful unto death, — these are indeed impressive and typical instances of loyalty; but they are not the only possible instances. Anybody who, for a time, is in charge of the lives of others (for instance, any one who takes a party of children on a pleasure trip) may have the opportunity to possess and to show as genuine a loyalty as does the true-hearted captain of the sinking ship. For danger is everywhere, and to be in charge of life is always an occasion for loyalty. Anybody who has friends may devote his life to some cause which his friendship defines for him and makes, in his eyes, sacred. Anybody who has given his word in a serious matter may come to think himself called upon to sacrifice every private advantage in order to keep his word. Thus, then, anything which can link various people by fixed social ties may suggest to somebody the opportunity for a lifelong loyalty. The loyal are, therefore, to be found in all orders of society. They may be of very various degrees of intelligence, of power, of effectiveness. Wherever there are mothers and brethren, and kindred of any degree, and social organizations of any type; wherever men accept offices, or pledge their word, or, as in the pursuit of science or of art, coöperate in the search for truth and for beauty, — there are to be found causes which may appeal to the loyal interest of somebody. Loyalty may thus exist amongst the lowliest and amongst the loftiest of mankind. The king and the peasant, the saint and the worldling, all have their various opportunities for loyalty. The practical man of the world and the seemingly lonely student of science may be equally loyal.

But whatever the cause to which one is loyal, and whoever it be that is loyal, the spirit of loyalty is always the one which our preliminary definition set forth, and which our former discussion attempted more precisely to describe. Whenever a cause, beyond your private self, greater than you are, — a cause social in its nature and capable of linking into one the wills of various individuals, a cause thus at once personal and, from the

purely human point of view, superpersonal, —
whenever, I say, such a cause so arouses your
interest that it appears to you worthy to be
served with all your might, with all your soul,
with all your strength, then this cause awakens
in you the spirit of loyalty. If you act out
this spirit, you become, in fact, loyal. And
upon the unity of this spirit, amidst all its
countless varieties, our future argument will
depend. It is essential to that argument to
insist that the humblest, as well as the wisest
and mightiest of men, may share in this one
spirit.

Now, loyalty, thus defined, is, as we have
maintained, something which we all, as human beings, need. That is, we all need to
find causes which shall awaken our loyalty.
I tried to indicate to you at the last time the
grounds for this our common need for loyalty.
In order to do so, I began with a confessedly
lower view of loyalty. I have asked you, for
the time, in this opening study, to abstract altogether from the cause to which any man is
loyal, to leave out of account whether that

cause is or is not in your opinion worthy, and to begin by considering what good the loyal man gets out of the personal attitude of loyalty, whatever be his cause. Only by thus beginning can we prepare the way for a higher view of loyalty.

Loyalty, I have said, be the cause worthy or unworthy, is for the loyal man a good, just as, even if his beloved be unworthy, love may in its place still be a good thing for a lover. And loyalty is for the loyal man not only a good, but for him chief amongst all the moral goods of his life, because it furnishes to him a personal solution of the hardest of human practical problems, the problem: "For what do I live? Why am I here? For what am I good? Why am I needed?"

The natural man, more or less vaguely and unconsciously, asks such questions as these. But if he looks merely within his natural self, he cannot answer them. Within himself he finds vague cravings for happiness, a chaos of desires, a medley of conflicting instincts. He has come —

"Into this universe, the why not knowing,
  Nor whence, like water, willy-nilly flowing."

He must, then, in any case consult society in order to define the purpose of his life. The social order, however, taken as it comes, gives him customs, employment, conventions, laws, and advice, but no one overmastering ideal. It controls him; but often by the very show of authority it also inflames his self-will. It rebukes and amuses; it threatens and praises him by turns; but it leaves him to find out and to justify the sense of his own life as he can. It solves for him no ultimate problems of life, so long as his loyalty is unawakened.

Only a cause, then, an absorbing and fascinating social cause, which by his own will and consent comes to take possession of his life, as the spirits that a magician summons might by the magician's own will and consent take control of the fortunes of the one who has called for their aid, — only a cause, dignified by the social unity that it gives to many human lives, but rendered also vital

58

for the loyal man by the personal affection which it awakens in his heart, only such a cause can unify his outer and inner world. When such unity comes, it takes in him the form of an active loyalty. Whatever cause thus appeals to a man meets therefore one of his deepest personal needs, and in fact the very deepest of his moral needs; namely, the need of a life task that is at once voluntary and to his mind worthy.

II

So far the former discussion led us. But already, at this point, an objection arises, — or rather, there arise a whole host of objections, — whereof I must take account before you will be ready to comprehend the philosophy of loyalty which I am to propose in later lectures. These objections, familiar in the present day, come from the partisans of certain forms of Individualism which in our modern world are so prevalent. I shall devote this lecture to a study of the relations of the spirit of loyalty to the spirit of individualism. Individualism is as Protean as loyalty. Hence my task involves meeting various very different objections.

Somewhat more than a year since, I was attempting to state in the presence of a company of young people my arguments for loyalty. I was trying to tell that company, as I am trying to tell you, how much we all need some form of loyalty as a centralizing motive in our personal lives. I was also deploring the fact that, in our modern American life, there are so many social motives that seem to take away from people the true spirit of loyalty, and to leave them distracted, unsettled as to their moral standards, uncertain why or for what they live. After I had said my word, my hearers were invited to discuss the question. Amongst those who responded was a very earnest youth, the son of a Russian immigrant. My words had awakened my young friend's righteous indignation. "Loyalty," so he in effect said, "has been in the past one of humanity's most disastrous failings and weaknesses. Tyrants have used the spirit of loyalty as their principal tool. I am glad," he went on, "that we are outgrowing loyalty, whatever its forms or whatever the causes that it serves. What we want in the future is the training of individual judgment. We want enlightenment and independence. Let us have done with loyalty."

I need hardly remark that my opponent's earnestness, his passion for the universal triumph of individual freedom, his plainness of speech, his hatred of oppression, were themselves symptoms of a very loyal spirit. For he had his cause. That was plain. It was a social cause, — the one need of the many for release from the oppressor. He spoke like a man who was devoted to that cause. I honored his loyalty to humanity, in so far as he understood the needs of his fellows. His spirit, then, as he spoke, simply illustrated my own thesis. He was awake, resolute, eager. He had his ideal. And his loyalty to the cause of the oppressed had given to him this fine self-possession. He was a living instance of my view of the value of loyalty to the loyal man.

So, in fact, he was not my opponent. But he thought that he was. And his view of loyalty, his conception that loyalty is by its nature, as a spirit of devotion and of self-sacrifice for a cause, necessarily a spirit of subservience, of slavish submission, — this view, I say, although it was clearly refuted by the very existence of his own loyalty to the cause of the relief of the people from the oppressor, was still a misunderstanding of himself and of life, — a misunderstanding such as is nowadays only too common. Here, then, is one form which current objections to the spirit of loyalty often take.

Another and a decidedly different objection to my own views about loyalty was expressed to me, also within the past year, by a friend high in official position in a distant community, — a teacher who has charge of many youth, and who is profoundly concerned for their moral welfare. "I wish," he said, "that, if you address the youth who are under my charge, you would tell them that loyalty to their various organizations, to their clubs, to their secret societies, to their own student body generally, is no excuse for mischief-makers, and gives to loyal students no right to encourage one another to do mischief, and then to stand together to shield offenders for the sake of loyalty. Loyalty hereabouts," he in substance went on, speaking of his own community, "is a cloak to cover a multitude of sins. What these youth need is the sense that each individual has his own personal duty, and should develop his own conscience, and should not look to loyalty to excuse him from individual responsibility."

The objection which was thus in substance contained in my friend's words, was of course partly an objection to the special causes to which these students were loyal; that is, it was an objection to their clubs, and to their views about the special rights of the student body. In so far, of course, this objection does not yet concern us; for I am not now estimating the worth of men's causes, but am considering only the inner value of the loyal spirit to the man who has that spirit, whatever be the cause to which this man is loyal. In part, however, this objection was founded upon a well-known form of ethical individualism, and is an objection that does here concern us. For his own good, so my critic seemed to hold, each man needs to develop his own individual sense of personal duty and of responsibility. Loyalty, as my critic further held, tends to take the life out of a young man's conscience, because it makes him simply look outside of himself to see what his cause requires him to do. In other words, loyalty seems to be opposed to the development of that individual auton-omy of the moral will which, as I told you in the last lecture, Kant insists upon, and which all moralists must indeed emphasize as one of our highest goods. If I look to my cause to tell me what to do, am I not resigning my moral birthright? Must I not always judge my own duty? Now, does not loyalty tend to make me ask my club or my other social cause simply to tell me what to do?

And yet, as you see, even the objector who

pointed out this difficulty about loyalty cannot have been as much my opponent as he seemed to believe that he was. For he himself, by virtue of his own autonomous choice of his career, is a very loyal teacher, devoted to his office, and loyal to the true welfare of his students as he sees that welfare. I am sure that his spirit must be the very loyalty which I have been describing to you. He is an independent sort of man, who has chosen his cause and is now profoundly loyal. Otherwise, how could he love, as he does, the hard tasks of his office and live, as he does, in his devotion to that office, accepting its demands as his own? He works like a slave at his own task, — and of course he works lovingly. Yet he seemed to condemn the loyalty of his students to their clubs as essentially slavish. Is there not some misunderstanding here?

But yet another, and once more a very different form of individualism I find, at times, opposed by my objectors to the loyalty whose importance I am maintaining. The objection here in question is familiar. It may be stated thus: The modern man —yes, the modern woman also, as we sometimes are told — can be content only with the completest possible self-development and the fullest self-expression which the conditions of our social life permit. We all of us have individual rights, so such an objector vigorously insists. Duties, perhaps, as he adds, we also occasionally have, under rather exceptional, perhaps abnormal and annoying, conditions. But whether or no the duties get in our way and hinder our growth, the rights at least are ours. Now, there is no good equal to winning what is your right; namely, this free self-expression, this untrammelled play of the spirit. You have opinions; utter them. They are opposed to current moral traditions; then so much the better; for when you utter them you know, because of their unconventional sound, that they must be your own. Even so, your social ties prove irksome. Break them. Form new ones. Is not the free spirit eternally young? From this point of view loyalty does indeed appear to be slavish. Why sacrifice the one thing that you have, — your chance to be yourself, and nobody else?

I need not further pursue, at the moment, the statement of the case for this special type of modern individualism. In this form individualism does not stand, like the enthusiasm of my young Russian, for sympathy with the oppressed, but rather for the exuberance of the vitality of certain people who, as I shall hereafter try to show, have not yet found out what to do with themselves. In any case, individualism of this sort, as I have said, is familiar enough. You know it well in recent literature. Plays, romances, essays, embody its teachings. You know this form of individualism also in real life. You read of its doings in the current newspapers. As you go about your own daily business, it sometimes, to show its moral dignity, jostles you more than even our modern congestion of population makes necessary; or it passes you by all too swiftly and perilously, in its triumphant and intrepid — self-assertion. In brief, the people who have more rights than duties have gained a notable and distinguished ethical position in our modern world. The selfish we had always with us. But the divine right to be selfish was never more ingeniously defended, in the name of the loftiest spiritual dignity, than it is sometimes defended and illustrated to-day.

But even now I have not done with stating the case of my objectors. Still another form of modern individualism exists, and this form is again very different from any of the foregoing forms. Yet once more I must let a friend of mine state the case for this sort of individualism. This is no longer the enthusiastic revolt against the oppressor which my young Russian expressed; nor is it the interest in moral independence of judgment which the teacher of youth emphasized; nor is it the type of self-assertion which prefers rights to duties; it is, on the contrary, the individualism of those who seek, and who believe that they find, an interior spiritual light which guides them and which relieves them of the need of any loyalty to externally visible causes. Such people might themselves sometimes speak of their fidelity to their inner vision as a sort of loyalty. But they would not define their loyalty in the terms which I have used in defining the loyal spirit. The friend of whom I have spoken stated the case for such people by saying: "Loyalty, such as you define, is not a man's chief good. Spirituality, contemplative self-possession, rest in the light of the truth, interior peace — these constitute, if one can attain to them, man's chief good. Good works for other men, and what externally appears as loyal conduct — such things may and will result from the attainment of inner perfection, but will so result merely because the good soul overflows, just as, to adapt the famous metaphor of Plotinus, just as the sun shines. The true good is to be at one with yourself within. Then you are at the centre of your world, and whatever good deeds you ought to do will result from the mere fact that you are thus self-possessed, and are therefore also in possession of light and peace. It is, then, spirituality rather than loyalty which we principally need." Thus, then, my friend's objection was stated.

I have thus let four different kinds of individualism state their case, as against my own thesis that loyalty is man's chief moral good. Perhaps the foregoing objections are the principal ones which my thesis in the present day has to meet; although, as I said, a host of special objections can be made merely by varying the form of these. The objections, as you will have observed, are founded upon very various and mutually conflicting principles. Yet each one of them seems somewhat formidable, especially at this stage of my argument, where I am maintaining, not that loyalty is good because or in so far as its cause is objectively and socially a good cause, but that loyalty is a centrally significant good for the loyal man himself, apart from the cause to which he is loyal, and so apart from the usefulness to other people which his loyalty may possess.

III

The scholastic philosopher, Thomas Aquinas, in his famous theological treatise, the Summa, always, in each one of the articles into which his work is divided, gives his opponents the word before he states his own case. And after thus setting forth in order the supposed reasons for the very views which he intends to combat, and immediately before beginning his detailed argument for the theses that he proposes to defend, he confronts his various opponents with some single counter-consideration, — a Scriptural passage, a word from the Fathers, or whatever brief assertion will serve his purpose, — as a sort of indication to all of his opponents together that they somehow must be in the wrong. This brief opening of his confutation is always formally introduced by the set phrase: *Sed contra est*, "But on the contrary stands the fact that," etc.

And so now, having sketched various objections, due to equally various forms of individualism, I may venture my own *Sed contra est* before I go on to a better statement of my case. Against all my four opponents stands the following fact: —

A little while since the Japanese won much

admiration from all of us by the absolute loyalty to their own national cause which they displayed during their late war. Hereupon we turned for information to our various authorities upon things Japanese, and came to know something of that old moral code Bushido which Nitobe in his little book has called the Soul of Japan. Well, whatever our other views regarding Japanese life and policy, I think that we have now come to see that the ideal of Bushido, the ancient Japanese type of loyalty, despite the barbarous life of feuds and of bloodshed in which it first was born, had very many elements of wonderful spiritual power about it. Now, Bushido did indeed involve many anti-individualistic features. But it never meant to those who believed in it any sort of mere slavishness. The loyal Japanese Samurai, as he is described to us by those who know, never lacked his own sort of self-assertion. He never accepted what he took to be tyranny. He had his chiefs; but as an individual, he was proud to serve them. He often used his own highly trained judgment regarding the applications of the complex code of honor under which he was reared. He was fond of what he took to be his rights as a man of honor. He made much, even childlike, display of his dignity. His costume, his sword, his bearing, displayed this sense of his importance. Yet his ideal at least, and in large part his practice, as his admirers depict him, involved a great deal of elaborate cultivation of a genuine spiritual serenity. His whole early training involved a repression of private emotions, a control over his moods, a deliberate cheer and peace of mind, all of which he conceived to be a necessary part of his knightly equipment. Chinese sages, as well as Buddhistic traditions, influenced his views of the cultivation of this interior self-possession and serenity of soul. And yet he was also a man of the world, a warrior, an avenger of insults to his honor; and above all, he was loyal. His loyalty, in fact, consisted of all these personal and social virtues together.

This Japanese loyalty of the Samurai was trained by the ancient customs of Bushido to such freedom and plasticity of conception and expression that, when the modern reform came, the feudal loyalties were readily transformed, almost at a stroke, into that active devotion of the individual to the whole nation and to its modern needs and demands, —that devotion, I say, which made the rapid and wonderful transformation of Japan possible. The ideal of Bushido, meanwhile, spread from the old military class to a great part of the nation at large. It is plainly not the only Japanese ideal. And I am not disposed to exaggerate what I hear of the part that the old Japanese loyalty actually plays in determining the present morality of the plain people of that country. But there can be no doubt that Bushido has been an enviable spiritual possession of vast numbers of Japanese. It is indeed universally agreed that this ideal of loyalty has been conceived in Japan as requiring a certain impersonalism, a certain disregard of the central importance of the ethical individual. And I myself do not believe, in fact, that the Japanese have rightly conceived the true worth of the individual. And yet, after all, is not this Japanese ideal of loyalty a sort of counter-instance which all the various opponents of loyalty, whose cases have heretofore been stated, ought to consider?

For Japanese loyalty has not been a mere tool for the oppressors to use. Herein it has indeed strongly differed from that blind and pathetic loyalty of the ignorant Russian peasant, which my young friend had in mind when he condemned loyalty. Japanese loyalty has led, on the contrary, to a wonderful and cordial solidarity of national spirit. If it has discouraged strident self-assertion, it has not suppressed individual judgment. For the modern transformation of Japan has surely depended upon a vast development of personal ingenuity and plasticity, not only intellectual but moral. This loyalty has not made machines out of men. It has given rise to a wonderful development of individual talent. Japanese loyalty, furthermore, if indeed strongly opposed to the individualism which knows its rights rather than its duties, has expressed itself in an heroic vigor of life which the most energetic amongst those who love to assert themselves might well envy. And meanwhile this loyalty, in some at least of its representatives, has included, has used, has elaborately trained an inner serenity of individual self-control, a spiritual peace and inner perfection which I find enviable, and which many of our own nervous wanderers upon the higher plane might find indeed restful if they could attain to it. There is, then, not so much opposition between the good which the loyal may win, and the various personal goods which our partisans of individualism emphasized. I do not believe that the Japanese ought to be our models. Our civilization has its own moral problems, and must meet them in its own way. But I am sure that our various partisans of ethical individualism, when they conceive that they are opponents of the spirit of loyalty, ought to consider those aspects of Japanese loyalty which most of us do indeed find enviable. This counter-instance serves to show that, at least in some measure, the various personal goods which the different ethical individualists seek, have been won, and so can be won, by means of the spirit of loyalty.

IV

With this counter-instance once before you, I may now go on to a closer analysis of the rational claims of ethical individualism.

Whether he takes account of the physical or of the natural world, every man inevitably finds himself as apparently occupying the centre of his own universe. The starry heavens form to his eyes a sphere, and he himself, so far as he can ever see, is at the centre of that sphere. Yes, the entire and infinite visible world, to be even more exact, seems to each of you to have its centre about where the bridge of your own nose chances to be. What is very remote from us we all of us find it difficult to regard as real in the same warm and vital sense in which the world near to us is real. It is for us all a little hard to see how the people who live far from our own dwelling-place, say, the Australians or the Siberians, can really fail to observe how distant they are from the place where, after all, it is from our point of view most natural to have one's abiding-place. And the people of alien races must surely feel, if they share our so natural insight regarding them, that they are indeed a strange sort of folk.

This inevitable illusion of perspective is, of course, responsible for what is called our natural selfishness. But on the other hand, this illusion is no mere illusion. It suggests, even while it distorts, the true nature of things. The real world has a genuine relation to the various personalities that live in it. The truth is diversified by its relation to these personalities. Values do indeed alter with the point of view. The world as interpreted by me is a fact different from the world as interpreted by you; and these different interpretations have all of them their basis in the truth of things. So far as moral values are concerned, it is therefore indeed certain that no ethical doctrine can be right which neglects individuals, and which disregards, I will not say their right, but their duty to centralize their lives, and so their moral universe, about their own purposes. As we seem to be at the centre of the starry heavens, so each of us is indeed at the centre of his own realm of duty. No impersonal moral theory can be successful. Individualism in ethics has therefore its permanent and, as I believe, its absolute justification in the nature of things. And the first principle of a true individualism in ethics is indeed that moral autonomy of any rational person which I mentioned at the last time, and which Kant so beautifully defended. Only your own will, brought to a true knowledge of itself, can ever determine for you what your duty is. And so far, then, I myself, in defending loyalty as a good thing for the loyal, am speaking as an ethical individualist. My whole case depends upon this fact. And so, in following my argument, you need not fear that I want to set some impersonal sort of life as an ideal over against the individualism of

the opponents of loyalty whose various cases I
have just been stating. I contend only that
their opposition to loyalty, their view that one's
individual purposes can be won otherwise than
by and through loyalty, is due merely to their
failure to comprehend what it is that the ethical
individual needs, and what it is that in all,
even of his blindest strivings, he is still seeking.
What I hold is, that he inevitably seeks his
own form of loyalty, his own cause, and his
opportunity to serve that cause, and that he
can actually and rationally find spiritual rest
and peace in nothing else. Let me indicate to
you my reasons for this view; and then, as
I hope, you will see that my opponents do not
at heart mean to oppose me. As the matter
stands, they merely oppose themselves, and
this through a mere misapprehension.

To my opponent, wherever he is, I therefore
say: Be an individual; seek your own individual good; seek that good thoroughly, un-
swervingly, unsparingly, with all your heart
and soul. But I persist in asking: Where, in
heaven above and in earth beneath, have you

to look for this your highest good? Where can you find it?

V

The first answer to this question might very naturally take the form of saying: "I seek, as my highest individual good, my own happiness." But, as I pointed out to you in my opening discussion, this answer only gives you your problem back again, unsolved. Happiness involves the satisfaction of desires. Your natural desires are countless and conflicting. What satisfies one desire defeats another. Until your desires are harmonized by means of some definite plan of life, happiness is therefore a mere accident. Now it comes and now it flies, you know not why. And the mere plan to be happy if you can is by itself no plan. You therefore cannot adopt the pursuit of happiness as your profession. The calling that you adopt will in any case be something that the social order in which you live teaches you; and all plans will in your mind be practically secondary to your general ·plan to live in some sort of tolerable relation to your social order. For you are indeed a social being.

If, next, you simply say: "Well, then, I will live as my social order requires me to live," — again, as we have seen, you find yourself without any determinate way of expressing your own individuality. For if the social order is indeed not as chaotic in its activities as by nature you yourself are, it is quite unable of itself to do more than to make of you, in one way or another, a link in its mechanism, or a member of one of its numerous herds, in any case a mere vehicle for carrying its various influences. Against this fate, as an ethical individual, you justly revolt. If this chance social existence furnishes to you your only plan of life, you therefore live in a sad but altogether too common wavering between blind submission and incoherent rebellion. As Kant says of the natural human being, your state so far remains this, that you can neither endure your fellow-man nor do without him. You do your daily work perhaps, but you complain of your employer. You earn your bread, but you are bitter because of hard times, and because of the social oppressions that beset you. You are insufferably dreary when alone, but are bored when in company. Your neighbors determine your customs; but in return for the art of life thus acquired, you persistently criticise your neighbors for their offences against custom. Imitation and jealousy, slavish conventionality, on the one hand, secret or open disorder, on the other, bickerings that inflame, and gayeties that do not cheer — these, along with many joys and sorrows that come by accident, constitute upon this level the chronicle of your life. It is such a chronicle that the daily newspapers, in the most of their less violently criminal reports, constantly rehearse to us, so far as they are not taken up with reporting the really greater social activities of mankind. Thus the merely social animal escapes from the chaos of his natural desires, only to sink to the pettiness of a hewer of wood and drawer of water for his lord, the social order. He may become fairly happy for a longer or shorter time; but that is so far mere chance. He may even think himself fairly contented, but that is, upon this level, mere callousness.

But if, indeed, you are a genuine individualist, you cannot accept this fate. If you are an effective individualist, you do not remain a prey to that fate. You demand your liberation. You require your birthright of the social order which has brought your individuality into being. You seek the salvation of yourself from this intolerable bondage. Now, I have already counselled you to seek such liberty in the form of loyalty; that is, of a willing and whole-souled devotion to a fascinating social cause. But perhaps this does not yet seem to you the solution. And therefore you may next turn to a very familiar form of individualism. You may say, "Well, then, my ideal shall be Power. I seek to be master of my fate."

That the highest good for the individual is to be defined in terms of Power, — this, I say, is a well-known doctrine. It is very old. It is in each generation renewed, for the young men define it ever afresh. In our time it has been emphasized by Nietzsche's view that the central principle of ethical individuality is *Der Wille zur Macht* — the will to be mighty.

If this is now your doctrine, the power that you seek will, of course, not be mere brute force. Those have ill interpreted Nietzsche, — that heavily burdened invalid, doomed to solitude by his sensitiveness, and yet longing amidst his sufferings for an influence over his fellow-men of which he never became conscious before the end came to him, — those have ill interpreted him who have found in his passionate aphorisms only a glorification of elemental selfishness. No, — power for Nietzsche, as for all ethical individualists of serious significance, is power idealized through its social efficacy, and conceived in terms of some more or less vague dream of a completely perfected and ideal, but certainly social, individual man. And Nietzsche's particular dream of power has all the pathos of the hopeless invalid's longing for escape from his disease. The tragedy of his personal life was one only of the countless tragedies to which the seekers after power have fallen victims.

Well, if it is power that you seek, your ideal may not be expressed as Nietzsche expressed his, but in any case you will be seeking some socially idealized type of power. Warriors, statesmen, artists, will be before your mind as examples of what power, if attained, would be. In your sphere you will be seeking to control social conditions, and to centre them about your individual interests. Our present question is: Can you hope to attain the highest individual good by such a quest for power as this?

When we remember that the principal theme of heroic tragedy in all ages has been the fate of the seekers after individual power, and that one of the favorite topics of comedy, from the beginning of comedy until to-day, has been the absurdity of the quest of these very lovers of power, our question begins to suggest its own answer. Regarding few topics have the sages, the poets, and the cynical critics of mankind more agreed than regarding the significance of the search for power, whenever power is sought otherwise than as a mere means to some more ideal goal. Let us then merely recall the well-known verdict that tragedy and comedy, and the wisdom of the ages, have passed upon the lust of power.

The objections to defining your individual good in terms merely of power are threefold. First, the attainment of power is a matter of fortune. Set your heart upon power, make it your central good in life, and you have staked the worth of your moral individuality upon a mere venture. In the end old age and death will at best make a mockery of whatever purely individual powers your life as a human being can possess for yourself alone. While life lasts, the attainment of power is at best but a little less uncertain than the attainment of a purely private individual happiness. This is the first objection to power as the highest individual good. It is an objection as sound as it is old; and in this objection the poets and the sages are at one; and the cynics join in the verdict.

Secondly, the lust for power is insatiable. To say, I seek merely power, not as a means to an end, but as my chief good, is to say that, for my own sake alone, I condemn myself to a laborious quest that is certain, from my own point of view and however fortune favors me, to give me a constantly increasing sense that I have not found what I need. Thus, then, I condemn myself to an endless disappointment. This objection is also well known; and it is easily illustrated. After fortune had long seemed to be actually unable to thwart Napoleon, he went on to destroy himself, merely because his lust for power grew with what it fed upon, until the fatal Russian campaign became inevitable.

Thirdly, in the often quoted words of Spinoza, "The power of man is infinitely surpassed by the power of external things;" and hence the seeker after merely individual power has undertaken a battle with the essentially irresistible forces of the whole universe. Therefore, to adapt other words of Spinoza, when such a seeker after power "ceases to suffer, he ceases also to be." The larger one's powers, the more are the places in which he comes in contact with the world that he would conquer, and the more are the ways in which he feels its force. It is with the seeker after individual power as it has lately been with some of our greater corporations. The vaster the capital of these corporations, and the more widely spread the interests that they control, the more numerous are their enemies, the harder the legislative enactments that they have to fear, the greater their fines if they are convicted of misdoing. Power means increasing opportunities for conflict. Hence the mere seeker for power not only, by the accidents of fortune, may meet his downfall, but also, himself, actively pursues his own destruction.

Whoever pursues power, and only power, wars therefore with unconquerable fate. But you may retort: "Are the loyal also not subject to fortune, like others?" And, in reply, I call at once attention to the fact that precisely such fate is what the loyal also unhesitatingly face; but they meet it in a totally different spirit. They, too, are indeed subject to fortune; their loyalty, also, is an insatiable passion to serve their cause; they also know what it is to meet with tasks that are too vast for mortals to accomplish. Only their very loyalty, since it is a willing surrender of the self to the cause, is no hopeless warfare with this fate, but is a joyous acceptance in advance of the inevitable destiny of every individual human being. In such matters, as you well know, "the readiness is all." Loyalty discounts death, for it is from the start a readiness to die for the cause. It defies fortune; for it says: "Lo, have I not surrendered my all? Did I ever assert that just I must be fortunate?" Since it views life as service of the cause, it is content with an endless quest. Since nothing is too vast to undertake for the cause, loyalty regards the greatness of its tasks as mere opportunity. But the lust of power, on the contrary, has staked its value not upon the giving up of self-will, but upon the attainment of private possessions, upon the winning of the hopeless fight of the individual with his private fate. Hence, in a world of wandering and of private disasters and unsettlement, the loyal indeed are always at home. For however they may wander or lose, they view their cause as fixed and as worthy. To serve the cause is an honor; and this honor they have in their own possession. But in this same world the seekers for power are never at home. If they have conquered Western Europe, power lies still hidden in the Far East, and they wander into the snows of a Russian winter in pursuit of that ghost of real life which always beckons to them from the dark world beyond. Napoleon's loyal soldiers won, indeed, their goal when they died in his service. But he lost. They were more fortunate than was their leader. They had their will, and then slept. He lived on for a while, and failed.

Such considerations may suffice to show wherein consists the blindness of those who in our day seem to themselves to have more rights than duties. This homily of mine about the vanity of the lust for power is, of course, a very old story. You may think these remarks but wearisome moral platitudes. But we all have to learn this sort of lesson sometime afresh, and for ourselves. And if the story of the fate of the lust for power is old, it is none the less true. And it is a story that we in America seem to need to have told to us anew to-day. Any financial crisis with its tragedies can serve by way of illustration.

But perhaps this is not the form of individualism which is asserted by the ethical individualist whom I am now addressing. Perhaps you say: "It is not mere power that I want. I demand moral autonomy, personal independence of judgment. I want to call my soul my own. The highest good is an active self-possession." Well, in this case I wholly agree with your demand, precisely in so far as you make that demand positive. I only undertake to supplement your own statement of your demand, and to oppose your denial of the supreme value of loyalty. For what end, I insist, is your moral independence good? Do you find anything finally important in the mere fact that you are unlike anybody else, or that you think good what another man condemns? What worth could you find in an independence that should merely isolate you, that should leave you but a queer creature, whose views are shared by nobody? No, — you are still a social being. What you really mean is, that you want to be heard and respected as regards your choice of your own cause. What you actually intend is, that nobody else shall determine, apart from this your own choice, the special loyalty that shall be yours.

Now, I, who have defined loyalty as the willing devotion of a self to a cause, am far from demanding from you any unwilling devotion to any cause. You are autonomous, of course. You can even cut loose from all loyalty if you will. I only plead that, if you do so, if you wholly decline to devote yourself to any cause whatever, your assertion of moral independence will remain but an empty proclaiming of a moral sovereignty over your life, without any definite life over which to be sovereign. For the only definite life that you can live will be a social life. This social life may indeed be one of enmity to society. But in that case your social order will crush you, and then your moral independence will die without any of the comfort of the loyal man's last glimpse of the banner for which he sheds his blood. For the loyal man's cause survives him. Your independence will die with you, and while it lives, nobody else will find its life worth insuring. Your last word will then be simply the empty phrase: "Lo, I asserted myself." But in the supposed case of your enmity to society, you will never know what it was that you thus asserted when you asserted yourself. For a man's self has no contents, no plans, no purposes, except those which are, in one way or another, defined for him by his social relations. Or, again, your life may indeed be one of social conformity, of merely conventional morality. But such a life you, as individualist, have learned to despise, — I think justly. Your only recourse, then, is to assert your autonomy by choosing a cause, and by loyally living, and, when need be, dying for that cause. Then you will not only assert yourself by your choice of a cause, but express yourself articulately by your service. The only way to be practically autonomous is to be freely loyal.

Such considerations serve to indicate my answer to those individualists who insist upon moral independence. My young Russian and my friend, the teacher, were individualists of this type. My answer to them both, as you see, is that the only coherent moral independence which you can define is one that has to find its expression in a loyal life. There is endless room, as we shall hereafter see, for a rational autonomy in your choice of your cause.

But you may still insist that one other form of individualism remains open to you. You may say: "I seek spirituality, serenity, an inward peace, which the world cannot give or take away. Therefore my highest good lies not in loyalty, but in this interior perfection." But once more I answer you with the whole verdict of human experience regarding the true nature of spiritual self-possession. You seek serenity. Yes, but you do not want your serenity to mean mere apathy. You seek peace, but you do not want dreamless sleep, nor yet the repose of a swoon. The stones seem to remain serene when you by chance stumble over them; some tropical islanders slumber peacefully in their huts when there is no work pressing. But the types of serenity that are for you in question are not of such sort. You are an ethical individualist. Your repose must therefore be the only repose possible to a being with a conscious and a vital will of his own. It must be the repose of activity; the assurance of one who lives energetically, even because he lives in the spirit. But in what spirit shall you live? Are you not a man? Can you live with an active will of your own without living amongst your brethren? Seek, then, serenity, but let it be the serenity of the devotedly and socially active being. Otherwise your spiritual peace is a mere feeling of repose, and, as such, contents at its best but one side of your nature, namely, the merely sensuous side. The massive sensation that all things are somehow well is not

the highest good of an active being. Even one
of the most typical of mystics, Meister Eckhart,
once stated his case, regarding a true spiritual
life, thus: "That a man should have a life of
rest and peace in God is good; that he should
bear a painful life with patience is better;
but that he should find his rest even in his painful life, that is best of all." Now, this last
state, the finding of one's rest and spiritual
fulfilment even in one's very life of toil itself, —
this state is precisely the state of the loyal,
in so far as their loyalty gets full control of
their emotional nature. I grant you that not
all the loyal are possessed of this serenity;
but that is because of their defects of nature
or of training. Their loyalty would be more
effective, indeed, if it were colored throughout
by the serenity that you pursue. But your own
peace of spirit will be meaningless unless it is
the peace of one who is willingly devoted to his
cause. "The loving," says Bayard Taylor, in
his lyric of Sebastópol, "the loving are the dar-
ing." And I say: The truly serene of spirit
are to be found at their best amongst the loyal.

In view of such considerations, when I listen to our modern ethical individualists, — to our poets, dramatists, essayists who glorify personal initiative — to our Walt Whitman, to Ibsen, and, above all, when I listen to Nietzsche, — I confess that these men move me for a time, but that erelong I begin to listen with impatience. Of course, I then say, be indeed autonomous. Be an individual. But for Heaven's sake, set about the task. Do not forever whet the sword of your resolve. Begin the battle of real individuality. Why these endless preliminary gesticulations? "Leave off thy — grimaces," and begin. There is only one way to be an ethical individual. That is to choose your cause, and then to serve it, as the Samurai his feudal chief, as the ideal knight of romantic story his lady, — in the spirit of all the loyal.

III

LOYALTY TO LOYALTY

LECTURE III

LOYALTY TO LOYALTY

THE two foregoing lectures have been devoted to defending the thesis that loyalty
is, for the loyal individual himself, a supreme
good, whatever be, for the world in general,
the worth of his cause. We are next to consider what are the causes which are worthy of
loyalty.

I

But before I go on to this new stage of our
discussion, I want, by way of summary of all
that has preceded, to get before your minds as
clear an image as I can of some representative
instance of loyalty. The personal dignity and
worth of a loyal character can best be appre-
ciated by means of illustrations. And I confess that those illustrations of loyalty which my
earlier lectures used must have aroused some
associations which I do not want, as I go on to

my further argument, to leave too prominent in your minds. I chose those instances because they were familiar. Perhaps they are too familiar. I have mentioned the patriot aflame with the war-spirit, the knight of romance, and the Japanese Samurai. But these examples may have too much emphasized the common but false impression that loyalty necessarily has to do with the martial virtues and with the martial vices. I have also used the instance of the loyal captain standing by his sinking ship. But this case suggests that the loyal have their duties assigned to them by some established and customary routine of the service to which they belong. And that, again, is an association that I do not want you to make too prominent. Loyalty is perfectly consistent with originality. The loyal man may often have to show his loyalty by some act which no mere routine predetermines. He may have to be as inventive of his duties as he is faithful to them.

Now, I myself have for years used in my own classes, as an illustration of the personal worth and beauty of loyalty, an incident of English history, which has often been cited as a precedent in discussions of the constitutional privileges of the House of Commons, but which, as I think, has not been sufficiently noticed by moralists. Let me set that incident now before your imagination. Thus, I say, do the loyal bear themselves: In January, 1642, just before the outbreak of hostilities between King Charles I and the Commons, the King resolved to arrest certain leaders of the opposition party in Parliament. He accordingly sent his herald to the House to demand the surrender of these members into his custody. The Speaker of the House in reply solemnly appealed to the ancient privileges of the House, which gave to that body jurisdiction over its own members, and which forbade their arrest without its consent. The conflict between the privileges of the House and the royal prerogative was herewith definitely initiated. The King resolved by a show of force to assert at once his authority; and, on the day following that upon which the demand sent through his herald had been refused, he went in person, accompanied by soldiers, to the House. Then, having placed his guards at the doors, he entered, went up to the Speaker, and, naming the members whom he desired to arrest, demanded, "Mr. Speaker, do you espy these persons in the House?"

You will observe that the moment was an unique one in English history. Custom, precedent, convention, obviously were inadequate to define the Speaker's duty in this most critical instance. How, then, could he most admirably express himself? How best preserve his genuine personal dignity? What response would secure to the Speaker his own highest good? Think of the matter merely as one of the Speaker's individual worth and reputation. By what act could he do himself most honor?

In fact, as the well-known report, entered in the Journal of the House, states, the Speaker at once fell on his knee before the King and said: "Your Majesty, I am the Speaker of this House, and, being such, I have neither eyes to see nor tongue to speak save as this

House shall command; and I humbly beg your Majesty's pardon if this is the only answer that I can give to your Majesty."

Now, I ask you not, at this point, to consider the Speaker's reply to the King as a deed having historical importance, or in fact as having value for anybody but himself. I want you to view the act merely as an instance of a supremely worthy personal attitude. The beautiful union of formal humility (when the Speaker fell on his knee before the King) with unconquerable self-assertion (when the reply rang with so clear a note of lawful defiance); the willing and complete identification of his whole self with his cause (when the Speaker declared that he had no eye or tongue except as his office gave them to him), — these are characteristics typical of a loyal attitude. The Speaker's words were at once ingenious and obvious. They were in line with the ancient custom of the realm. They were also creative of a new precedent. He had to be inventive to utter them; but once uttered, they seem almost commonplace in their plain truth.

The King might be offended at the refusal; but he could not fail to note that, for the moment, he had met with a personal dignity greater than kingship, — the dignity that any loyal man, great or humble, possesses whenever he speaks and acts in the service of his cause.

Well — here is an image of loyalty. Thus, I say, whatever their cause, the loyal express themselves. When any one asks me what the worthiest personal bearing, the most dignified and internally complete expression of an individual is, I can therefore only reply: Such a bearing, such an expression of yourself as the Speaker adopted. Have, then, your cause, chosen by you just as the Speaker had chosen to accept his office from the House. Let this cause so possess you that, even in the most thrilling crisis of your practical service of that cause, you can say with the Speaker: "I am the servant of this cause, its reasonable, its willing, its devoted instrument, and, being such, I have neither eyes to see nor tongue to speak save as this cause shall command." Let this be your bearing, and this your deed.

Then, indeed, you know what you live for. And you have won the attitude which constitutes genuine personal dignity. What an individual in his practical bearing can be, you now are. And herein, as I have said, lies for you a supreme personal good.

II

With this image of the loyal self before us, let us now return to the main thread of our discourse. We have deliberately declined, so far, to consider what the causes are to which men ought to be loyal. To turn to this task is the next step in our philosophy of loyalty.

Your first impression may well be that the task in question is endlessly complex. In our opening lecture we defined indeed some general characteristics which a cause must possess in order to be a fitting object of loyalty. A cause, we said, is a possible object of loyalty only in case it is such as to join many persons into the unity of a single life. Such a cause, we said, must therefore be at once personal, and, for one who defines personality from a purely human point of view, superpersonal. Our initial illustrations of possible causes were, first, a friendship which unites several friends into some unity of friendly life; secondly, a family, whose unity binds its members' lives together; and, thirdly, the state, in so far as it is no mere collection of separate citizens, but such an unity as that to which the devoted patriot is loyal. As we saw, such illustrations could be vastly extended. All stable social relations may give rise to causes that may call forth loyalty.

Now, it is obvious that nobody can be equally and directly loyal to all of the countless actual social causes that exist. It is obvious also that many causes which conform to our general definition of a possible cause may appear to any given person to be hateful and evil causes, to which he is justly opposed. A robber band, a family engaged in a murderous feud, a pirate crew, a savage tribe, a Highland robber clan of the old days — these might constitute causes to which somebody has been, or is, profoundly loyal. Men have loved such causes devotedly, have served them for a lifetime.

Yet most of us would easily agree in thinking such causes unworthy of anybody's loyalty. Moreover, different loyalties may obviously stand in mutual conflict, whenever their causes are opposed. Family feuds are embittered by the very strength of the loyalty of both sides. My country, if I am the patriot inflamed by the war-spirit, seems an absolutely worthy cause; but my enemy's country usually seems hateful to me just because of my own loyalty; and therefore even my individual enemy may be hated because of the supposed baseness of his cause. War-songs call the individual enemy evil names just because he possesses the very personal qualities that, in our own loyal fellow-countrymen, we most admire. "No refuge could save the hireling and slave." Our enemy, as you see, is a slave, because he serves his cause so obediently. Yet just such service we call, in our own country's heroes, the worthiest devotion.

Meanwhile, in the foregoing account of loyalty as a spiritual good to the loyal man, we have insisted that true loyalty, being a willing devotion of the self to its cause, involves some element of autonomous choice. Tradition has usually held that a man ought to be loyal to just that cause which his social station determines for him. Common sense generally says, that if you were born in your country, and still live there, you ought to be loyal to that country, and to that country only, hating the enemies across the border whenever a declaration of war requires you to hate them. But we have declared that true loyalty includes some element of free choice. Hence our own account seems still further to have complicated the theory of loyalty. For in answering in our last lecture the ethical individualists who objected to loyalty, we have ourselves deliberately given to loyalty an individualistic coloring. And if our view be right, and if tradition be wrong, so much the more difficult appears to be the task of defining wherein consists that which makes a cause worthy of loyalty for a given man, since tradition alone is for us an insufficient guide.

To sum up, then, our apparent difficulties,

they are these: Loyalty is a good for the loyal man; but it may be mischievous for those whom his cause assails. Conflicting loyalties may mean general social disturbances; and the fact that loyalty is good for the loyal does not of itself decide whose cause is right when various causes stand opposed to one another. And if, in accordance with our own argument in the foregoing lecture, we declare that the best form of loyalty, for the loyal individual, is the one that he freely chooses for himself, so much the greater seems to be the complication of the moral world, and so much the more numerous become the chances that the loyalties of various people will conflict with one another.

III

In order to overcome such difficulties, now that they have arisen in our way, and in order to discover a principle whereby one may be guided in choosing a right object for his loyalty, we must steadfastly bear in mind that, when we declared loyalty to be a supreme good for the loyal man himself, we were not speaking of a good that can come to a few men only — to heroes or to saints of an especially exalted mental type. As we expressly said, the mightiest and the humblest members of any social order can be morally equal in the exemplification of loyalty. Whenever I myself begin to look about my own community to single out those people whom I know to be, in the sense of our definition, especially loyal to their various causes, I always find, amongst the most exemplary cases of loyalty, a few indeed of the most prominent members of the community, whom your minds and mine must at once single out because their public services and their willing sacrifices have made their loyalty to their chosen causes a matter of common report and of easy observation. But my own mind also chooses some of the plainest and obscurest of the people whom I chance to know, the most straightforward and simple-minded of folk, whose loyalty is even all the more sure to me because I can certainly affirm that they, at least, cannot be making any mere display of loyalty in order that they should be seen of men. Nobody knows of their loyalty except those who are in more or less direct touch with them; and these usually appreciate this loyalty too little. You all of you similarly know plain and wholly obscure men and women, of whom the world has never heard, and is not worthy, but who have possessed and who have proved in the presence of you who have chanced to observe them, a loyalty to their chosen causes which was not indeed expressed in martial deeds, but which was quite as genuine a loyalty as that of a Samurai, or as that of Arnold von Winkelried when he rushed upon the Austrian spears. As for the ordinary expressions of loyalty, not at critical moments and in the heroic instants that come to the plainest lives, but in daily business, we are all aware how the letter carrier and the housemaid may live, and often do live, when they choose, as complete a daily life of steadfast loyalty as could any knight or king. Some of us certainly know precisely such truly great personal embodiments of loyalty in those who are, in the world's ill-judging eyes, the little ones of the community.

Now these facts, I insist, show that loyalty is in any case no aristocratic gift of the few. It is, indeed, too rare a possession to-day in our own American social order; but that defect is due to the state of our present moral education. We as a nation, I fear, have been forgetting loyalty. We have been neglecting to cultivate it in our social order. We have been making light of it. We have not been training ourselves for it. Hence we, indeed, often sadly miss it in our social environment. But all sound human beings are made for it and can learn to possess it and to profit by it. And it is an essentially accessible and practical virtue for everybody.

This being true, let us next note that all the complications which we just reported are obviously due, in the main, to the fact that, as loyal men at present are, their various causes, and so their various loyalties, are viewed by them as standing in mutual, sometimes in deadly conflict. In general, as is plain if somebody's loyalty to a given cause, as for instance to a family, or to a state, so expresses itself as to involve a feud with a neighbor's family, or a warlike assault upon a foreign state, the result is obviously an evil; and at least part of the reason why it is an evil is that, by reason of the feud or the war, a certain good, namely, the enemy's loyalty, together with the enemy's opportunity to be loyal, is assailed, is thwarted, is endangered, is, perhaps, altogether destroyed. If the loy-alty of A is a good for him, and if the loyalty of B is a good for him, then a feud between A and B, founded upon a mutual conflict between the causes that they serve, obviously involves this evil, namely, that each of the combatants assails, and perhaps may altogether destroy, precisely what we have seen to be the best spiritual possession of the other, namely, his chance to have a cause and to be loyal to a cause. The militant loyalty, indeed, also assails, in such a case, the enemy's physical comfort and well-being, his property, his life; and herein, of course, militant loyalty does evil to the enemy. But if each man's having and serving a cause is his best good, the worst of the evils of a feud is the resulting attack, not upon the enemy's comfort or his health or his property or his life, but upon the most precious of his possessions, his loyalty itself.

If loyalty is a supreme good, the mutually destructive conflict of loyalties is in general a supreme evil. If loyalty is a good for all sorts and conditions of men, the war of man against man has been especially mischievous, not so much because it has hurt, maimed, impoverished, or slain men, as because it has so often robbed the defeated of their causes, of their opportunities to be loyal, and sometimes of their very spirit of loyalty.

If, then, we look over the field of human life to see where good and evil have most clustered, we see that the best in human life is its loyalty; while the worst is whatever has tended to make loyalty impossible, or to destroy it when present, or to rob it of its own while it still survives. And of all things that thus have warred with loyalty, the bitterest woe of humanity has been that so often it is the loyal themselves who have thus blindly and eagerly gone about to wound and to slay the loyalty of their brethren. The spirit of loyalty has been misused to make men commit sin against this very spirit, holy as it is. For such a sin is precisely what any wanton conflict of loyalties means. Where such a conflict occurs, the best, namely, loyalty, is used as an instrument in order to compass the worst, namely, the destruction of loyalty.

It is true, then, that some causes are good, while some are evil. But the test of good and evil in the causes to which men are loyal is now definable in terms which we can greatly simplify in view of the foregoing considerations.

If, namely, I find a cause, and this cause fascinates me, and I give myself over to its service, I in so far attain what, for me, if my loyalty is complete, is a supreme good. But my cause, by our own definition, is a social cause, which binds many into the unity of one service. My cause, therefore, gives me, of necessity, fellow-servants, who with me share this loyalty, and to whom this loyalty, if complete, is also a supreme good. So far, then, in being loyal myself, I not only get but give good; for I help to sustain, in each of my fellow-servants, his own loyalty, and so I help him to secure his own supreme good. In so far, then, my loyalty to my cause is also a loyalty to my fellows' loyalty. But now suppose that my cause, like the family in a feud, or like the pirate ship, or like the aggressively warlike nation, lives by the destruction of the loyalty of other families, or of its own community, or of other communities. Then, indeed, I get a good for myself and for my fellow-servants by our common loyalty; but I war against this very spirit of loyalty as it appears in our opponent's loyalty to his own cause.

And so, a cause is good, not only for me, but for mankind, in so far as it is essentially a *loyalty to loyalty*, that is, is an aid and a furtherance of loyalty in my fellows. It is an evil cause in so far as, despite the loyalty that it arouses in me, it is destructive of loyalty in the world of my fellows.. My cause is, indeed, always such as to involve some loyalty to loyalty, because, if I am loyal to any cause at all, I have fellow-servants whose loyalty mine supports. But in so far as my cause is a predatory cause, which lives by overthrowing the loyalties of others, it is an evil cause, because it involves disloyalty to the very cause of loyalty itself.

IV

In view of these considerations, we are now able still further to simplify our problem by laying stress upon one more of those very features which seemed, but a moment since, to complicate the matter so hopelessly. Loyalty, as we have defined it, is the willing devotion of a self to a cause. In answering the ethical individualists, we have insisted that all of the higher types of loyalty involve autonomous choice. The cause that is to appeal to me at all must indeed have some elemental fascination for me. It must stir me, arouse me, please me, and in the end possess me. Moreover, it must, indeed, be set before me by my social order as a possible, a practically significant, a living cause, which binds many selves in the unity of one life. But, nevertheless, if I am really awake to the significance of my own moral choices, I must be in the position of accepting this cause, as the Speaker of the House, in the incident that I have narrated, had freely accepted his Speakership. My cause cannot be merely forced upon me. It is I who make it my own. It is I who willingly say: "I have no eyes to see nor tongue to speak save as this cause shall command." However much the cause may seem to be assigned to me by my social station, I must coöperate in the choice of the cause, before the act of loyalty is complete.

Since this is the case, since my loyalty never is my mere fate, but is always also my choice, I can of course determine my loyalty, at least to some extent, by the consideration of the actual good and ill which my proposed cause does to mankind. And since I now have the main criterion of the good and ill of causes before me, I can define a principle of choice which may so guide me that my loyalty shall become a good, not merely to myself, but to mankind.

This principle is now obvious. I may state it thus: In so far as it lies in your power, so choose your cause and so serve it, that, by reason of your choice and of your service, there shall be more loyalty in the world rather than less. And, in fact, so choose and so serve your individual cause as to secure thereby the greatest possible increase of loyalty amongst men. More briefly: *In choosing and in serving the cause to which you are to be loyal, be, in any case, loyal to loyalty.*

This precept, I say, will express how one should guide his choice of a cause, in so far as he considers not merely his own supreme good, but that of mankind. That such autonomous choice is possible, tends, as we now see, not to complicate, but to simplify our moral situation. For if you regard men's loyalty as their fate, if you think that a man must be loyal simply to the cause which tradition sets before him, without any power to direct his own moral attention, then indeed the conflict of loyalties seems an insoluble problem; so that, if men find themselves loyally involved in feuds, there is no way out. But if, indeed, choice plays a part, — a genuine even if limited part, in directing the individual's choice of the cause to which he is to be loyal, then indeed this choice may be so directed that loyalty to the universal loyalty of all mankind shall be furthered by the actual choices which each enlightened loyal person makes when he selects his cause.

V

At the close of our first discussion we supposed the question to be asked, Where, in all our complex and distracted modern world, in which at present cause wars with cause, shall we find a cause that is certainly worthy of our loyalty? This question, at this very moment, has received in our discussion an

answer which you may feel to be so far provisional, — perhaps unpractical, — but which
you ought to regard as, at least in principle,
somewhat simple and true to human nature.
Loyalty is a good, a supreme good. If I myself could but find a worthy cause, and serve it
as the Speaker served the House, having neither eyes to see nor tongue to speak save as
that cause should command, then my highest
human good, in so far as I am indeed an active
being, would be mine. But this very good of
loyalty is no peculiar privilege of mine; nor
is it good only for me. It is an universally
human good. For it is simply the finding of
a harmony of the self and the world, — such
a harmony as alone can content any human
being.

In these lectures I do not found my argument upon some remote ideal. I found
my case upon taking our poor passionate
human nature just as we find it. This "eager
anxious being" of ours, as Gray calls it, is
a being that we can find only in social ties,
and that we, nevertheless, can never fulfil

without a vigorous self-assertion. We are by nature proud, untamed, restless, insatiable in our private self-will. We are also imitative, plastic, and in bitter need of ties. We profoundly want both to rule and to be ruled. We must be each of us at the centre of his own active world, and yet each of us longs to be in harmony with the very outermost heavens that encompass, with the lofty orderliness of their movements, all our restless doings. The stars fascinate us, and yet we also want to keep our own feet upon our solid human earth. Our fellows, meanwhile, overwhelm us with the might of their customs, and we in turn are inflamed with the naturally unquenchable longing that they should somehow listen to the cries of our every individual desire.

Now this divided being of ours demands reconciliation with itself; it is one long struggle for unity. Its inner and outer realms are naturally at war. Yet it wills both realms. It wants them to become one. Such unity, however, only loyalty furnishes to us, — loyalty, which finds the inner self intensified and exalted even by the very act of outward looking and of upward looking, of service and obedience,—loyalty, which knows its eyes and its tongue to be never so much and so proudly its own as when it earnestly insists that it can neither see nor speak except as the cause demands,—loyalty, which is most full of life at the instant when it is most ready to become weary, or even to perish in the act of devotion to its own. Such loyalty unites private passion and outward conformity in one life. This is the very essence of loyalty. Now loyalty has these characters in any man who is loyal. Its emotions vary, indeed, endlessly with the temperaments of its adherents; but to them all it brings the active peace of that rest in a painful life,—that rest such as we found the mystic, Meister Eckhart, fully ready to prize.

Loyalty, then, is a good for all men. And it is in any man just as much a true good as my loyalty could be in me. And so, then, if indeed I seek a cause, a worthy cause, what cause could be more worthy than the cause of loyalty to loyalty; that is, the cause of making loyalty prosper amongst men? If I could serve that cause in a sustained and effective life, if some practical work for the furtherance of universal human loyalty could become to me what the House was to the Speaker, then indeed my own life-task would be found; and I could then be assured at every instant of the worth of my cause by virtue of the very good that I personally found in its service.

Here would be for me not only an unity of inner and outer, but an unity with the unity of all human life. What I sought for myself I should then be explicitly seeking for my whole world. All men would be my fellow-servants of my cause. In principle I should be opposed to no man's loyalty. I should be opposed only to men's blindness in their loyalty, I should contend only against that tragic disloyalty to loyalty which the feuds of humanity now exemplify. I should preach to all others, I should strive to practise myself, that active mutual furtherance of universal loyalty which is what humanity obviously most needs, if indeed loyalty, just as the willing devotion of a self to a cause, is a supreme good.

And since all who are human are as capable of loyalty as they are of reason, since the plainest and the humblest can be as true-hearted as the great, I should nowhere miss the human material for my task. I should know, meanwhile, that if indeed loyalty, unlike the "mercy" of Portia's speech, is not always mightiest in the mightiest, it certainly, like mercy, becomes the throned monarch better than his crown. So that I should be sure of this good of loyalty as something worthy to be carried, so far as I could carry it, to everybody, lofty or humble.

Thus surely it would be humane and reasonable for me to define my cause to myself, — if only I could be assured that there is indeed some practical way of making loyalty to loyalty the actual cause of my life. Our question therefore becomes this: Is there a practical way of serving the universal human cause of loyalty to loyalty? And if there is such a way, what is it? Can we see how personally so to act that we bring loyalty on earth to a fuller fruition, to a wider range of efficacy, to a more effective sovereignty over the lives of men? If so, then indeed we can see how to work for the cause of the genuine kingdom of heaven.

VI

Yet I fear that as you have listened to this sketch of a possible and reasonable cause, such as could be a proper object of our loyalty, you will all the while have objected: This may be a definition of à possible cause, but it is an unpractical definition. For what is there that one can do to further the loyalty of mankind in general? Humanitarian efforts are an old story. They constantly are limited in their effectiveness both by the narrowness of our powers, and by the complexity of the human nature which we try to improve. And if any lesson of philanthropy is well known, it is this, that whoever tries simply to help mankind as a whole, loses his labor, so long as he does not first undertake to help those nearest to him. Loyalty to the cause of universal loyalty — how, then, shall it constitute any practical working scheme of life?

I answer at once that the individual man, with his limited powers, can indeed serve the cause of universal loyalty only by limiting his undertakings to some decidedly definite personal range. He must have his own special and personal cause. But this cause of his can indeed be chosen and determined so as to constitute a deliberate effort to further universal loyalty. When I begin to show you how this may be, I shall at once pass from what may have seemed to you a very unpractical scheme of life, to a realm of familiar and commonplace virtuous activities. The only worth of my general scheme will then lie in the fact that, in the light of this scheme, we can, as it were, see the commonplace virtues transfigured and glorified by their relation to the one highest cause of all. My thesis is *that all the commonplace virtues, in so far as they are indeed defensible and effective, are special forms of loyalty to loyalty,* and are to be justified, centralized, inspired, by the one supreme effort to do good, namely, the effort to make loyalty triumphant in the lives of all men.

The first consideration which I shall here insist upon is this: Loyalty, as we have all along seen, depends upon a very characteristic and subtle union of natural interest, and of free choice. Nobody who merely follows his natural impulses as they come is loyal. Yet nobody can be loyal without depending upon and using his natural impulses. If I am to be loyal, my cause must from moment to moment fascinate me, awaken my muscular vigor, stir me with some eagerness for work, even if this be painful work. I cannot be loyal to barren abstractions. I can only be loyal to what my life can interpret in bodily deeds. Loyalty has its elemental appeal to my whole organism. My cause must become one with my human life. Yet all this must occur not without my willing choice. I must control my devotion. It will possess me, but not without my voluntary complicity; for I shall accept the possession. It is, then, with the cause to which you personally are loyal, as it was with divine grace in an older theology. The cause must control you, as divine grace took saving control of the sinner; but only your own will can accept this control, and a grace that merely compels can never save.

Now that such an union of choice with natural interest is possible, is a fact of human nature, which every act of your own, in your daily calling, may be used to exemplify. You cannot do steady work without natural interest; but whoever is the mere prey of this passing interest does no steady work. Loyalty is a perfect synthesis of certain natural desires, of some range of social conformity, and of your own deliberate choice.

In order to be loyal, then, to loyalty, I must indeed first choose forms of loyal conduct which appeal to my own nature. This means that, upon one side of my life, I shall have to behave much as the most unenlightened of the loyal do. I shall serve causes such as my natural temperament and my social opportunities suggest to me. I shall choose friends whom I like. My family, my community, my country, will be served partly because I find it interesting to be loyal to them.

Nevertheless, upon another side, all these my more natural and, so to speak, accidental loyalties, will be controlled and unified by a deliberate use of the principle that, whatever my cause, it ought to be such as to further, so far as in me lies, the cause of universal loyalty. Hence I shall not permit my choice of my special causes to remain a mere chance. My causes must form a system. They must constitute in their entirety a single cause, my life of loyalty. When apparent conflicts arise amongst the causes in which I am interested, I shall deliberately undertake, by devices which we shall hereafter study in these lec-, so reduce the conflict to the greatest possible harmony. Thus, for instance, I may say, to one of the causes in which I am naturally bound up: —

> " I could not love thee, dear, so much,
> Loved I not honour more."

And in this familiar spirit my loyalty will aim to be, even within the limits of my own personal life, an united, harmonious devotion, not to various conflicting causes, but to one system of causes, and so to one cause.

Since this one cause is my choice, the cause of my life, my social station will indeed suggest it to me. My natural powers and preferences will make it fascinating to me, and yet I will never let mere social routine, or mere social tradition, or mere private caprice, impose it upon me. I will be individualistic in my loyalty, carefully insisting, however, that whatever else I am, I shall be in all my practical activity a loyal individual, and, so far as in me lies, one who chooses his personal causes for the sake of the spread of universal loyalty. Moreover, my loyalty will be a growing loyalty. Without giving up old loyalties I shall annex new ones. There will be evolution in my loyalty.

The choice of my cause will in consequence be such as to avoid unnecessary conflict with the causes of others. So far I shall indeed negatively show loyalty to loyalty. It shall not be my cause to destroy other men's loyalty. Yet since my cause, thus chosen and thus organized, still confines me to my narrow personal range, and since I can do so little directly for mankind, you may still ask whether, by such a control of my natural interests, I am indeed able to do much to serve the cause of universal loyalty.

Well, it is no part of the plan of this discourse to encourage illusions about the range of influence that any one poor mortal can exert. But that by the mere force of my practical and personal loyalty, if I am indeed loyal, I am doing something for the cause of universal loyalty, however narrow my range of deeds, this a very little experience of the lives of other people tends to teach me. For who, after all, most encourages and incites me to loyalty? I answer, any loyal human being, whatever his cause, so long as his cause does not arouse my hatred, and does not directly injure my chance to be loyal. My fellow's special and personal cause need not be directly mine. Indirectly he inspires me by the very contagion of his loyalty. He sets me the example. By his loyalty he shows me the worth of loyalty. Those humble and obscure folk of whom I have before spoken, how precious they are to us all as inspiring examples, because of their loyalty to their own.

From what men, then, have I gained the best aid in discovering how to be myself loyal? From the men whose personal cause is directly and consciously one with my own? That is indeed sometimes the case. But others, whose personal causes were apparently remote in very many ways from mine, have helped me to some of my truest glimpses of loyalty.

For instance: There was a friend of my own youth whom I have not seen for years, who once faced the choice between a scholarly career that he loved, on the one hand, and a call of honor, upon the other, — who could have lived out that career with worldly success if he had only been willing to conspire with his chief to deceive the public about a matter of fact, but who unhesitatingly was loyal to loyalty, who spoke the truth, who refused to conspire, and who, because his chief was a plausible and powerful man, thus deliberately wrecked his own worldly chances once for all, and retired into a misunderstood obscurity in order that his fellow-men might henceforth be helped to respect the truth better. Now, the worldly career which that friend thus sacrificed for the sake of his loyalty is far from mine; the causes that he has since loyally served have not of late brought him near to me in worldly doings. I am not sure that we should ever have kept our interests in close touch with one another even if we had lived side by side. For he was and is a highly specialized type of man, austere, and a little disposed, like many scholars, to a life apart. For the rest, I have never myself been put in such a place as his was when he chose to make his sacrifice, and have never had his great choice set before me. Nor has the world rewarded him at all fairly for his fidelity. He is, then, as this world goes, not now near to me and not a widely influential man. Yet I owe him a great debt. He showed me, by the example of his free sacrifice, a good in loyalty which I might otherwise have been too blind to see. He is a man who does not love flattery. It would be useless for me now to offer to him either words of praise or words of comfort. He made his choice with a single heart and a clear head, and he has always declined to be praised. But it will take a long time, in some other world, should I meet him in such a realm, to tell him how much I owe to his example, how much he inspired me, or how many of his fellows he had indirectly helped to their own loyalty. For I believe that a good many others besides myself indirectly owe far more to him than he knows, or than they know. I believe that certain standards of loyalty and of scientific truthfulness in this country are to-day higher than they were because of the self-surrendering act of that one devoted scholar.

Loyalty, then, is contagious. It infects not only the fellow-servant of your own special cause, but also all who know of this act.

Loyalty is a good that spreads. Live it and you thereby cultivate it in other men. Be faithful, then, so one may say, to the loyal man; be faithful over your few things, for the spirit of loyalty, secretly passing from you to many to whom you are a stranger, may even thereby make you unconsciously ruler over many things. Loyalty to loyalty is then no unpractical cause. And you serve it not by becoming a mere citizen of the world, but by serving your own personal cause. We set before you, then, no unpractical rule when we repeat our moral formula in this form: Find your own cause, your interesting, fascinating, personally engrossing cause; serve it with all your might and soul and strength; but so choose your cause, and so serve it, that thereby you show forth your loyalty to loyalty, so that because of your choice and service of your cause, there is a maximum of increase of loyalty amongst your fellow-men.

VII

Yet herewith we have only begun to indicate how the cause of loyalty to loyalty may be made a cause that one can practically, efficaciously, and constantly serve. Loyalty, namely, is not a matter merely of to-day or of yesterday. The loyal have existed since civilization began. And, even so, loyalty to loyalty is not a novel undertaking. It began to be effective from the time when first people could make and keep a temporary truce during a war, and when first strangers were regarded as protected by the gods, and when first the duties of hospitality were recognized. The way to be loyal to loyalty is therefore laid down in precisely the rational portion of the conventional morality which human experience has worked out.

Herewith we approach a thesis which is central in my whole philosophy of loyalty. I announced that thesis in other words in the opening lecture. My thesis is that *all those duties which we have learned to recognize as the fundamental duties of the civilized man, the duties that every man owes to every man, are to be rightly interpreted as special instances of loyalty to loyalty.* In other words, all the recognized virtues can be defined in terms of our concept of loyalty. And this is why I assert that, when rightly interpreted, loyalty is the whole duty of man.

For consider the best-known facts as to the indirect influence of certain forms of loyal conduct. When I speak the truth, my act is directly an act of loyalty to the personal tie which then and there binds me to the man to whom I consent to speak. My special cause is, in such a case, constituted by this tie. My fellow and I are linked in a certain unity, — the unity of some transaction which involves our speech one to another. To be ready to speak the truth to my fellow is to have, just then, no eye to see and no tongue to speak save as this willingly accepted tie demands. In so far, then, speaking the truth is a special instance of loyalty. But whoever speaks the truth, thereby does what he then can do to help everybody to speak the truth. For he acts so as to further the general confidence of man in man. How far such indirect influence may extend, no man can predict.

Precisely so, in the commercial world, honesty in business is a service, not merely and not mainly to the others who are parties to the single transaction in which at any one time this faithfulness is shown. The single act of business fidelity is an act of loyalty to that general confidence of man in man upon which the whole fabric of business rests. On the contrary, the unfaithful financier whose disloyalty is the final deed that lets loose the avalanche of a panic, has done far more harm to general public confidence than he could possibly do to those whom his act directly assails. Honesty, then, is owed not merely and not even mainly to those with whom we directly deal when we do honest acts; it is owed to mankind at large, and it benefits the community and the general cause of commercial loyalty.

Such a remark is in itself a commonplace; but it serves to make concrete my general thesis that every form of dutiful action is a case of loyalty to loyalty. For what holds thus of truthfulness and of commercial honesty holds,

I assert, of every form of dutiful action. Each such form is a special means for being, by a concrete deed, loyal to loyalty.

We have sought for the worthy cause; and we have found it. This simplest possible of considerations serves to turn the chaotic mass of separate precepts of which our ordinary conventional moral code consists into a system unified by the one spirit of universal loyalty. By your individual deed you indeed cannot save the world, but you can at any moment do what in you lies to further the cause which both for you and for the human world constitutes the supreme good, namely, the cause of universal loyalty. Herein consists your entire duty.

Review in the light of this simple consideration, the usually recognized range of human duties. How easily they group themselves about the one principle: *Be loyal to loyalty.*

Have I, for instance, duties to myself? Yes, precisely in so far as I have the duty to be actively loyal at all. For loyalty needs not only a willing, but also an effective servant.

My duty to myself is, then, the duty to provide my cause with one who is strong enough and skilful enough to be effective according to my own natural powers. The care of health, self-cultivation, self-control, spiritual power — these are all to be morally estimated with reference to the one principle that, since I have no eyes to see or tongue to speak save as the cause commands, I will be as worthy an instrument of the cause as can be made, by my own efforts, out of the poor material which my scrap of human nature provides. The highest personal cultivation for which I have time is thus required by our principle. But self-cultivation which is not related to loyalty is worthless.

Have I private and personal rights, which I ought to assert? Yes, precisely in so far as my private powers and possessions are held in trust for the cause, and are, upon occasion, to be defended for the sake of the cause. My rights are morally the outcome of my loyalty. It is my right to protect my service, to maintain my office, and to keep my own merely in order that I may use my own as the cause commands. But rights which are not determined by my loyalty are vain pretence.

As to my duties to my neighbors, these are defined by a well-known tradition in terms of two principles, justice and benevolence. These two principles are mere aspects of our one principle. Justice means, in general, fidelity to human ties in so far as they are ties. Justice thus concerns itself with what may be called the mere forms in which loyalty expresses itself. Justice, therefore, is simply one aspect of loyalty — the more formal and abstract side of loyal life. If you are just, you are decisive in your choice of your personal cause, you are faithful to the loyal decision once made, you keep your promise, you speak the truth, you respect the loyal ties of all other men, and you contend with other men only in so far as the defence of your own cause, in the interest of loyalty to the universal cause of loyalty, makes such contest against aggression un-

144

avoidable. All these types of activity, within the limits that loyalty determines, are demanded if you are to be loyal to loyalty. Our principle thus at once requires them, and enables us to define their range of application. But justice, without loyalty, is a vicious formalism.

Benevolence, on the other hand, is that aspect of loyalty which directly concerns itself with your influence upon the inner life of human beings who enjoy, who suffer, and whose private good is to be affected by your deeds. Since no personal good that your fellow can possess is superior to his own loyalty, your own loyalty to loyalty is itself a supremely benevolent type of activity. And since your fellow-man is an instrument for the furtherance of the cause of universal loyalty, his welfare also concerns you, in so far as, if you help him to a more efficient life, you make him better able to be loyal. Thus benevolence is an inevitable attendant of loyalty. And the spirit of loyalty to loyalty enables us to define wherein consists a wise benevolence. Benevolence without loyalty is a dangerous sentimentalism. Thus viewed, then, loyalty to universal loyalty is indeed the fulfilment of the whole law.

IV

CONSCIENCE

LECTURE IV

CONSCIENCE

ONE of the main purposes of these lectures is to simplify our conceptions of duty and of the good. When I am in a practical perplexity, such as often arises in daily life, that friend can best advise me who helps me to ignore useless complications, to see simply and directly, to look at the central facts of my situation. And even so, when a moralist attempts a rational theory of duty, he ought, like the practical adviser of a friend in perplexity, to do what he can to rid our moral situation of its confusing complications. In these lectures I am trying to accomplish this end by centralizing our duties about the one conception of loyalty.

I

Conventional morality, as it is usually taught to us, consists of a maze of precepts. Some of these precepts we have acquired through the influence of Christianity. Some of them are distinctly unchristian, or even antichristian. Whatever their origin, whether Christian or Greek or barbarian, they lie side by side in our minds; and sometimes they tend to come into conflict with one another. Be just; but also be kind. Be generous; but also be strict in demanding what is your due. Live for others; but be careful of your own dignity, and assert your rights. Love all mankind; but resent insults, and be ready to slay the enemies of your country. Take no thought for the morrow; but be careful to save and to insure. Cultivate yourself; but always sacrifice yourself. Forget yourself; but never be so thoughtless in conduct that others shall justly say, "You have forgotten yourself." Be moderate in all things; but know no moderation in your devotion to righteousness. Such are a few of the well-known paradoxes of our popular morality. And these paradoxes are, for the most part, no mere accidents. Nearly all of these apparently conflicting moral maxims express some significant truth. What we want is a method of finding our way through the maze, a principle that shall unify our moral life, and that shall enable us to solve its paradoxes.

Such a centralizing and unifying principle we tried to propose at the last lecture. Our topic in the foregoing discussion was the question: By what criterion may we know that a proposed cause is one which is worthy of our loyalty? We answered the question by asserting that there is in any case *one* cause which is worthy of every man's loyalty. And that is the cause of loyalty itself. Do what you can to make men loyal, and to keep them in a loyal attitude; this was the sense of the general precept that we derived from our study of the value of loyalty to those who are loyal. Whoever follows this precept inevitably defines for himself a cause, and becomes loyal to that cause. His sovereign and central moral maxim may otherwise be stated thus: *Be loyal to loyalty.*

Our reasons for asserting that this maxim

is a sound guide to dutiful action were these: First, the primal fact that loyalty, in any man who possesses it, is his supreme good. Secondly, the further fact that such loyalty is not a good which only a few are able to get, — an aristocratic possession of a small company of saints; but it is, on the contrary, a good which is accessible to all sorts and conditions of men, so far as they have normal human interests and normal self-control. We saw that there is no sort of wholesome human life which does not furnish opportunities for loyalty. And whoever is loyal wins, whatever his social station, and precisely in so far as he is loyal, the same general form of spiritual fulfilment, namely, self-possession through self-surrender. The keeper of a lonely lighthouse and the leader of a busy social order, the housemaid and the king, have almost equal opportunities to devote the self to its own chosen cause, and to win the good of such devotion. In consequence of these two considerations, whoever undertakes to further the general cause of loyalty, is certainly aiming at the supreme

good of mankind at large. His cause, therefore, is certainly a worthy cause.

Nor is the undertaking to further the general cause of loyalty itself an unpractical
undertaking, — a vague philanthropy. On
the contrary, of all the efforts that you can
make on behalf of your fellow-men, the effort
to make them loyal to causes of their own is
probably the most generally and widely prac-
ticable. It is notoriously hard, by any direct
philanthropic effort, to give good fortune to any
man, except to some few of those with whose
fortunes you are most closely linked. Certain
forms of suffering can be relieved by the hospi-
tals, or by private skill and kindness. But
when the sufferer is relieved, he stands once
more merely on the threshold of life, and the
question, What can you do to give him life itself? is not yet answered. If, hereupon, you try
to make your fellow-man prosperous, by offer-
ing to him unearned good fortune, you may in
fact merely teach him to be wasteful and in-
dolent. If you seek to deal out happiness to
him by devices of your own, you find that he

generally prefers to look for happiness in his own way. If you attempt to give him contentment, you come into conflict with his insatiable natural desires.

But if you undertake to make him loyal, there is indeed much that you can do. For, as I pointed out at the close of the last lecture, all of what common sense rightly regards as your ordinary duties to mankind may be viewed, and ought to be viewed, as practically effective ways of helping on the cause of general loyalty. Thus, you can speak the truth to your fellow, and can thereby help him to a better confidence in mankind. This confidence in mankind will aid him in turn to speak the truth himself. And in truth-speaking there will be for him much real peace, for truth-speaking is a form of loyalty and will aid him to be otherwise loyal to his own. Precisely so, there are as many other ways of helping him to be loyal as there are other such obvious and commonly recognized duties to be done in your ordinary and peaceful dealings with him.

Let me mention one further instance that was not used amongst our illustrations at the last meeting: The true value of courtesy in ordinary human intercourse lies in the fact that courtesy is one expression of loyalty to loyalty, and helps every one who either receives or witnesses courtesy to assume himself a loyal attitude towards all the causes that are represented by the peaceful and reasonable dealings of man with man. The forms of courtesy, in fact, are largely derived from what once were, or still are, more or less ceremonious expressions of loyal devotion. Courtesy, then, may be defined as an explicit assumption of a loyal bearing. To adopt such a bearing with a real sincerity of heart is to express, in your passing actions, loyalty to universal loyalty. To act thus towards your individual fellow-man is then and there to help all who know of your act to be loyal. Courtesy, then, is a duty owed not so much to the individual to whom you are courteous, as to humanity at large.

There are, then, many ways of aiding your

fellow-man to be loyal. Now, as we also set forth at the last lecture, one of the most effective of these ways lies in being loyal yourself to some personally chosen and determinate social cause which constitutes your business. This special cause need not be one in which the particular fellow-man whom you are just now to help is, at the moment, directly interested. Your very loyalty to your own cause will tend to prove infectious. Whoever is loyal to his own therefore helps on the cause of universal loyalty by his every act of devotion, precisely in so far as he refrains from any hostile attack upon the loyalty of other people, and simply lets his example of loyalty work. Whoever makes the furtherance of universal loyalty his cause, lacks, therefore, neither practical means nor present opportunity for serving his cause.

To each man our principle therefore says: *Live in your own way a loyal life and one subject to the general principle of loyalty to loyalty.* Serve your own cause, but so choose it and so serve it that in consequence of your life loyalty amongst men shall prosper. Fortune may indeed make the range of your choice of your calling very narrow. Necessity may bind you to an irksome round of tasks. But sweeten these with whatever loyalty you can consistently get into your life. Let loyalty be your pearl of great price. Sell all the happiness that you possess or can get in disloyal or in non-loyal activities, and buy that pearl. When you once have found, or begun to find, your personal cause, be as steadily faithful to it as loyalty to loyalty henceforth permits. That is, if you find that a cause once chosen does indeed involve disloyalty to loyalty, as one might find who, having sworn fidelity to a leader, afterwards discovered his leader to be a traitor to the cause of mankind, you may have altogether to abandon the cause first chosen. But never abandon a cause except for the sake of some higher or deeper loyalty such as actually requires the change.

Meanwhile, the principle of loyalty to loyalty obviously requires you *to respect loyalty in all men, wherever you find it.* If your fellow's cause has, in a given case, assailed your own, and if, in the world as it is, conflict is inevitable, you may then have to war with your fellow's cause, in order to be loyal to your own. But even then, you may never assail whatever is sincere and genuine about his spirit of loyalty. Even if your fellow's cause involves disloyalty to mankind at large, you may not condemn the loyalty of your fellow in so far as it is loyalty. You may condemn only his blindly chosen cause. All the loyal are brethren. They are children of one spirit. Loyalty to loyalty involves the active furtherance of this spirit wherever it appears. Fair play in sport, chivalrous respect for the adversary in war, tolerance of the sincere beliefs of other men, — all these virtues are thus to be viewed as mere variations of loyalty to loyalty. Prevent the conflict of loyalties when you can, minimize such conflict where it exists, and, by means of fair play and of the chivalrous attitude towards the opponent, utilize even conflict, where it is inevitable, so as to further the cause of loyalty to loyalty. Such maxims are obvious consequences of our principle. Do we not gain, then, a great deal from our principle in the way of unifying our moral code?

II

But next, as to those just-mentioned paradoxes of popular morality, do we not gain from our principle a guide to help us through the maze? "Be just; but also be kind." These two precepts, so far as they are sound, merely emphasize, as we pointed out at the close of our last lecture, two distinct but inseparable aspects of loyalty. My cause links my fellow and myself by social ties which, in the light of our usual human interpretation of life, appear to stand for superpersonal interests, — for interests in property rights, in formal obligations, in promises, in various abstractly definable relations. If I am loyal, I respect these relations. And I do so since, from the very definition of a cause to which one can be loyal, this cause will become nothing unless these ties are preserved intact. But to respect relations as such is to be what men call just. Meanwhile, our common cause also personally interests both my fellow and myself. So far as we both know the cause, we love it, and delight in it. Hence in being loyal to our cause, I am also being kind to my fellow. For hereby I further his delight in just so far as I help him to insight. But kindness which is not bound up with loyalty is as a sounding brass and as a tinkling cymbal, a mere sentimentalism. And abstract justice, apart from loyalty, is a cruel formalism. My fellow wants to be loyal. This is his deepest need. If I am loyal to that need, I therefore truly delight him. But kindness that is not bound up with loyalty may indeed amuse my fellow for a moment. Yet like "fancy," such kindness "dies in the cradle where it lies." Even so, if I am loyal, I am also just. But justice that is no aspect of loyalty has no reason for existence. The true relations of benevolence and justice can therefore be best defined in terms of our conception of loyalty.

If any one says, "I will show thee my justice or my kindness without my loyalty," the loyal man may rightly respond, "I will show thee my kindness and my justice by my loyalty."

In a similar fashion, the moral problems regarding the right relations of strictness to generosity, of prudent foresight to present confidence, of self-surrender to self-assertion, of love to the righteous resistance of enemies, — all these moral problems, I say, are best to be solved in terms of the principle of loyalty to loyalty. As to the problem of the true concern and regard for the self, the loyal man cultivates himself, and is careful of his property rights, just in order to furnish to his cause an effective instrument; but he aims to forget precisely so much of himself as is, at any time, an obstruction to his loyalty; and he also aims to be careless of whatever about his private fortunes may be of no importance to his service of the cause. When he asserts himself, he does so because he has neither eyes to see nor tongue to speak save as his cause commands; and it is of precisely such self-sacrificing self-assertion that the foes of his cause would do well to beware. All the paradoxes about the care of self and the abandonment of self are thus soluble in terms of loyalty. Whoever knows and possesses the loyal attitude, *ipso facto* solves these paradoxes in each special case as it arises. And whoever comprehends the nature of loyalty to loyalty, as it is expressed in the form of fair play in sport, of chivalry in war, of tolerance in belief, and of the spirit that seeks to prevent the conflict of loyalties where such prevention is possible, — whoever, I say, thus comprehends what loyalty to loyalty means, holds the key to all the familiar mysteries about the right relation of the love of man to the strenuous virtues, and to the ethics of conflict.

III

As you see, it is my deliberate intention to maintain that the principle of loyalty to loyalty is a sufficient expression of what common sense calls "the dictates of conscience." When I state this thesis, it leads me, however, to a somewhat new question, which the title of this lecture is intended to emphasize.

Stated practically, this our next question takes the form of asking: Is the principle of loyalty to loyalty not only a means of solving certain perplexities, but an actually general, safe, and sufficient test of what is right and wrong in the doubtful moral situations which may arise in daily life? We have shown that the well-recognized duties and virtues, such as those which have to do with truth-speaking, with courtesy, with fair play in sport, and with chivalrous regard for enemies, can indeed be regarded, if we choose, as special forms of loyalty to loyalty. But it is indeed one thing (as you may now interpose) to interpret in terms of our principle certain virtues or duties that we already recognize. It is another thing to use the concept of loyalty to loyalty as an universal means of finding out what it is right to do when one is otherwise in doubt. Is our principle always a serviceable practical guide? Or, to use the well-known term, does our principle adequately express what people usually mean by the "dictates of conscience"?

The word "conscience," which here becomes important for our philosophy of loyalty, is a term of many uses. The problem as to the true nature of the human conscience is a complicated and difficult one. I shall here deal with the matter only in so far as is necessary for our own distinctly practical purpose. In expounding my precept, *Be loyal to loyalty*, I have set forth what does indeed pretend to be a general guiding maxim for conduct. But most of us, when we say, "My conscience dictates this or this sort of conduct," are not disposed to think of conscience as definable in terms of any one maxim. Our conscience seems to us to represent, in our ordinary lives, a good many related but nevertheless distinct motives, such as prudence, charity, reasonableness, piety, and so on. Conscience also seems to us somewhat mysterious in many of its demands, so that we often say, "I do not precisely know why this or this is right; but I feel sure that it is right, for my

conscience tells me so." Since, then, conscience seems so complex and sometimes so
mysterious a power, you may naturally hesitate to accept the views of a moralist who
attempts, as you may think, to simplify too
much the requirements of conscience. You
may still insist that the moral doctrine which
I have so far set forth is in one respect like all
other philosophies of conduct that fill the
history of ethical thought; because, as you
may insist, this theory is powerless to tell
any one what to do when a really perplexing
case of conscience arises.

The reproach that moral philosophers have
fine-sounding principles to report, but can
never tell us how these principles practically
apply, except when the cases are such as
common sense has already decided, — this is
an old objection to philosophical ethics. I
want to show you how I myself meet that
objection, and in what way, and to what extent,
as I think, the principle of loyalty to loyalty
does express the true dictates of conscience,
and does tell us what to do in doubtful cases.

What is conscience? You will all agree that the word names a mental possession of ours which enables us to pass some sort of judgment, correct or mistaken, upon moral questions as they arise. My conscience, then, belongs to my mental equipment, and tells me about right and wrong conduct. Moreover, my conscience approves or disapproves my conduct, excuses me or accuses me. About the general nature and office of the conscience we all of us, as I suppose, so far agree. Our differences regarding our conscience begin when questions arise of the following sort: Is our conscience inborn? Is it acquired by training? Are its dictates the same in all men? Is it God-given? Is it infallible? Is it a separate power of the mind? Or is it simply a name for a collection of habits of moral judgment which we have acquired through social training, through reasoning, and through personal experience of the consequences of conduct?

IV

In trying to meet these questions so far as they here concern us, it is important next to note a few fundamental features which characterize the personal life of all of us. The first of these features appears if one, instead of stopping with the question, "What is my conscience?" goes deeper still and asks the question, "Who and what am I?" This latter question also has indeed countless aspects, and a complete answer to it would constitute an entire system of metaphysics. But for our present purpose it is enough to note that I cannot answer the question, "Who am I?" except in terms of some sort of statement of the plans and purposes of my life. In responding to the question, "Who are you?" a man may first mention his name. But his name is a mere tag. He then often goes on to tell where he lives, and where he comes from. His home and his birthplace, however, are already what one may call purposeful aspects of his personality. For dwelling-place, country, birthplace, and similar incidental facts about a man tend to throw light upon his personality mainly because they are of importance for a further knowledge of his social relations, and so of his social uses and activities.

But the answer to the question, "Who are you?" really begins in earnest when a man mentions his calling, and so actually sets out upon the definition of his purposes and of the way in which these purposes get expressed in his life. And when a man goes on to say, "I am the doer of these and these deeds, the friend of these friends, the enemy of these opposing purposes, the member of this family, the one whose ideals are such and such, and are so and so expressed in my life," the man expresses to you at length whatever is most expressible and worth knowing in answer to the question, "Who are you?"

To sum up, then, I should say that a person, an individual self, may be defined as a human life lived according to a plan. If a man could live with no plan at all, purposelessly and quite passively, he would in so far be an organism, and also, if you choose, he would be a psychological specimen, but he would be no personality.   Wherever there is personality, there are purposes worked out in life.   If, as often happens, there are many purposes connected with the life of this human creature, many plans in this life, but no discoverable unity and coherence of these plans, then in so far there are many glimpses of selfhood, many fragmentary selves present in connection with the life of some human organism.   But there is so far no one self, no one person discoverable.   You are one self just in so far as the life that goes on in connection with your organism has some one purpose running through it.   By the terms " this person " and " this self," then, we mean this human life in so far as it expresses some one purpose.   Yet, of course, this one purpose which is expressed in the life of a single self need not be one which is defined by this self in abstract terms.   On the contrary, most of us are aware that our lives are unified, after a fashion, by the very effort that we more or less vaguely make to assert ourselves somehow as individuals in our world. Many of us have not yet found out how it would be best to assert ourselves. But we are trying to find out. This very effort to find out gives already a certain unity of purpose to our lives.

But in so far as we have indeed found out some cause, far larger than our individual selves, to which we are fully ready to be loyal, this very cause serves to give the required unity to our lives, and so to determine what manner of self each of us is, even though we chance to be unable to define in abstract terms what is the precise nature of this very cause. Loyalty may be sometimes almost dumb; it is so in many of those obscure and humble models of loyalty of whom I have already spoken. They express their loyalty clearly enough in deeds. They often could not very well formulate it in words. They could not give an abstract account of their business. Yet their loyalty gives them a business. It unifies their activities. It makes of each of these loyal beings an individual self, — a life unified by a purpose. This purpose may in such cases come to consciousness merely as a willing hunger to serve the cause, a proud obedience to the ideal call. But in any case, wherever loyalty is, there is selfhood, personality, individual purpose embodied in a life.

And now, further, if the argument of our first and second lectures is right, wherever a human selfhood gets practically and consciously unified, there is some form of loyalty. For, except in terms of some sort of loyal purpose, as we saw, this mass of instincts, of passions, of social interests, and of private rebelliousness, whereof the nature of any one of us is originally compounded, can never get any effective unity whatever.

To sum up so far, — a self is a life in so far as it is unified by a single purpose. Our loyalties furnish such purposes, and hence make of us conscious and unified moral persons. Where loyalty has not yet come to any sort of definiteness, there is so far present only a kind of inarticulate striving to be an individual self. This very search for one's true self is already a sort of life-purpose, which, as far as it goes, individuates the life of the person in question, and gives him a task. But loyalty brings the individual to full moral self-consciousness. It is devoting the self to a cause that, after all, first makes it a rational and unified self, instead of what the life of too many a man remains,—namely, a cauldron of seething and bubbling efforts to be somebody, a cauldron which boils dry when life ends.

V

But what, you may now ask, has all this view of the self to do with conscience? I answer that the nature of conscience can be understood solely in terms of such a theory of the self as the one just sketched.

Suppose that I am, in the foregoing sense, a more or less completely unified and loyal self. Then there are two aspects of this selfhood which is mine. I live a life; and I have, as a loyal being, an ideal. The life itself is not the ideal. They are and always remain in some sense distinct. For no one act of my life, and no limited set of acts of mine, can ever completely embody my ideal. My ideal comes to me from my cause, as the ideal of the Speaker of the House of Commons, in the story that we have already used to illustrate loyalty, came to him from the House. My cause, however, is greater than my individual life. Hence it always sets before me an ideal which demands more of me than I have yet done,— more, too, than I can ever at any one instant accomplish. Even because of this vastness of my ideal, even because that to which I am loyal is so much greater than I ever become, even because of all this can my ideal unify my life, and make a rational self of me.

Hence, if I am indeed one self, my one ideal is always something that stands over against my actual life; and each act of this life has to be judged, estimated, determined, as to its moral value, in terms of the ideal. My cause, therefore, as it expresses itself to my own consciousness through my personal ideal,— my cause and my ideal taken together, and viewed as one, perform the precise function which tradition has attributed to conscience. My cause, then, for our philosophy of loyalty, *is* my conscience, — my cause as interpreted through my ideal of my personal life. When I look to my cause, it furnishes me with a conscience; for it sets before me a plan or ideal of life, and then constantly bids me contrast this plan, this ideal, with my transient and momentary impulses.

To illustrate: Were I a loyal judge on the bench, whose cause was my official function, then my judicial conscience would be simply my whole ideal as a judge, when this ideal was contrasted with any of my present and narrower views of the situation directly before me. If, at a given moment, I tended to lay unfair stress upon one side of a controversy that had been brought into my court, my ideal would say: But a judge is impartial. If I were disposed to decide with inadvised haste, the ideal would say: But a judge takes account of the whole law bearing on the case. If I were offered bribes, my judicial conscience would reject them as being once for all ideally intolerable. In order to have such a judicial conscience, I should, of course, have to be able to view my profession as the carrying out of some one purpose, and so as one cause. This purpose I should have learned, of course, from the traditions of the office. But I should have had willingly to adopt these traditions as my own, and to conceive my own life in terms of them, in order to have a judicial conscience of my own. Analogous comments could be made upon the conscience of an artist, of a statesman, of a friend, or of a devoted member of a family, of any one who has a conscience. To have a conscience, then, is to have a cause, to unify your life by means of an ideal determined by this cause, and to compare the ideal and the life.

If this analysis is right, your conscience is simply that ideal of life which constitutes your moral personality. In having your conscience you become aware of your plan of being yourself and nobody else. Your conscience presents to you this plan, however, in so far as the plan or ideal in question is distinct from the life in which you are trying to embody your plan. Your life as it is lived, your experiences, feelings, deeds, — these are the embodiment of your ideal plan, in so far as your ideal plan for your own individual life as this self, gets embodied at all.

But no one act of yours ever expresses your plan of life perfectly. Since you thus always have your cause beyond you, there is always more to do. So the plan or ideal of life comes to stand over against your actual life as a general authority by which each deed is to be tested, just as the judicial conscience of the judge on the bench tests each of his official acts by comparing it with his personal ideal of what a judge should be. My conscience, therefore, is the very ideal that makes me this rational self, the very cause that inspires and that unifies me. Viewed as something within myself, my conscience is the spirit of the self, first moving on the face of the waters of natural desire, and then gradually creating the heavens and the earth of this life of the individual man. This spirit informs all of my true self, yet is nowhere fully expressed in any deed.

So that, in so far as we contrast the ideal with the single deed, we judge ourselves, condemn ourselves, or approve ourselves.

Our philosophy of loyalty thus furnishes us with a theory of a certain kind of consciousness which, in any case, precisely fulfils the functions of the traditional conscience. I need hardly say that the conscience which I have now described is not in its entirety at all innate. On the contrary, it is the flower rather than the root of the moral life. But unquestionably we should never get it unless we possessed an innate power to become reasonable, unless we were socially disposed beings, unless we were able so to develop our reason and our social powers as to see that the good of mankind is indeed also our own good, and, in brief, unless we inherited a genuine moral nature.

With this view of the nature of conscience, what can we say as to the infallibility of such a conscience? I answer: My conscience is precisely as fallible or as infallible as my choice of a cause is subject to error, or is of such nature as to lead me aright. Since loyalty, in so far, as it is loyalty, is always a good, the conscience of any loyal self is never wholly a false guide. Since loyalty may be in many respects blind, one's conscience also may be in many respects misleading. On the other hand, your conscience, at any stage of its development, is unquestionably the best moral guide that you then have, simply because, so far as it is viewed as an authority outside of you, it is your ideal, your cause, set before you; while, in so far as it is within you, it is the spirit of your own self, the very ideal that makes you any rational moral person whatever. Apart from it you are a mere pretence of moral personality, a manifold fermentation of desires. And as you have only your own life to live, your conscience alone can teach you how to live that life. But your conscience will doubtless grow with you, just as your loyalty and your cause will grow. The best way to make both of them grow is to render up your life to their service and to their expression.

Conscience, as thus defined, is for each of us a personal affair. In so far as many of us are fellow-servants of the same cause, and, above all, in so far as all of us, if we are enlightened, are fellow-servants of the one cause of universal loyalty, we do indeed share in the same conscience. But in so far as no two of us can live the same life, or be the same individual human self, it follows that no two of us can possess identical consciences, and that no two of us should wish to do so. Your conscience is not mine; yet I share with you the same infinite realm of moral truth, and we are subject to the same requirement of loyalty to loyalty. This requirement must interpret itself to us all in endlessly varied ways. The loyal are not all monotonously doing the same thing. Yet they individually partake of the one endlessly varied and manifold spirit of loyalty.

As to whether conscience is in any sense divine, we shall learn something in our closing lecture upon the relations of Loyalty and Religion.

VI

So far as is needful for our present practical purpose, the theory of the conscience which our philosophy of loyalty requires is now before you. We needed this theory in order to prepare the way for answering the question: In how far does the law, *Be loyal to loyalty*, enable us to decide cases of moral doubt? In how far does this principle furnish a means of discovering these special precepts about single cases which common sense calls the "dictates of conscience"?

How do moral doubts arise in the mind of a loyal person? I answer: Moral doubts arise in the loyal mind when there is an apparent conflict between loyalties. As a fact, that cause, which in any sense unifies a life as complex as my human life is, must of course be no perfectly simple cause. By virtue of my nature and of my social training, I belong to a family, to a community, to a calling, to a state, to humanity. In order to be loyal to loyalty, and in order to be a person at all, I must indeed unify my loyalty. In the meantime, however, I must also choose special causes to serve; and if these causes are to interest me, if they are to engross and to possess me, they must be such as together appeal to many diverse sides of my nature; they must involve me in numerous and often conflicting social tasks; they can form one cause only in so far as they constitute an entire system of causes. My loyalty will be subject, therefore, to the ancient difficulty regarding the one and the many. Unless it is one in its ultimate aim, it will be no loyalty to universal loyalty; unless it is just to the varied instincts and to the manifold social interests of a being such as I am, it cannot engross me.

Despite this great difficulty, however, the loyal all about us show us that this union of one and many in life is, at least in great portions of long human careers, a possible thing. We never completely win the union; we never realize to the full the one loyal life; but in so far as we are loyal, we win enough of this unity of life to be able to understand the ideal, and to make it our own guide. Our question still remains, however, this: Since the only loyal life that we can undertake to live is so complex, since the one cause of universal loyalty can only be served, by each of us, in a personal life wherein we have to try to unify various special loyalties, and since, in many cases, these special loyalties seem to us to conflict with one another, — how shall we decide, as between two apparently conflicting loyalties, which one to follow? Does our principle tell us what to do when loyalties thus seem to us to be in conflict with one another?

It is, of course, not sufficient to answer here that loyalty to loyalty requires us to do whatever can be done to harmonize apparently conflicting loyalties, and to remove the conflict of loyalties from the world, and to utilize even conflict, where it is inevitable, so as to further general loyalty. That answer we have already considered in an earlier passage of this discussion. It is a sound answer; but it does not meet those cases where conflict is forced upon us, and where we ourselves must take sides, and must annul or destroy one or two conflicting loyalties. One or two illustrations of such a type will serve to show what sorts of moral doubts our own philosophy of loyalty has especially to consider.

At the outset of our Civil War, many men of the border states, and many who had already been in the service of the Union, but who were conscious of special personal duties to single states of the Union, found themselves in presence of a well-known conflict of loyalties. Consider the personal problem that the future General Lee had to solve. Could the precept, *Be loyal to loyalty, and to that end, choose your own personal cause and be loyal thereto,* — could this principle, you may say, have been of any service in deciding for Lee his personal problem at the critical moment?

Or again, to take a problem such as some of my own students have more than once urged, in various instances, as a test case for my theory of loyalty to decide: A young woman, after a thorough modern professional training, begins a career which promises not only worldly success, but general good to the community in which she works. She is heartily loyal to her profession. It is a beneficent profession. She will probably make her mark in that field if she chooses to go on. Meanwhile she is loyal to her own family. And into the home, which she has left for her work, disease, perhaps death, enters. Her younger brothers and sisters are now unexpectedly in need of such care as hers; or the young family of her elder brother or sister, through the death of their father or mother, has come to be without due parental care. As elder sister or as maiden aunt this young woman could henceforth devote herself to family tasks that would mean very much for the little ones in question. But this devotion would also mean years of complete absorption in these family tasks, and would also mean an entire abandonment of the profession so hopefully begun, and of all the good that she can now be fairly sure of doing if she continues in that field.

What are the dictates of conscience? How shall this young woman solve her problem? How shall she decide between these conflicting loyalties? To be loyal to the family, to the needs of brothers, sisters, nephews, nieces, — surely this is indeed devotion of a self to a cause. But to be loyal to her chosen profession, which, in this case, is no mere hope, but which is already an actual and successful task, —is not that also loyalty to a cause? And does the principle, *Be loyal to loyalty*, decide which of these two causes is the one for this young woman to serve?

These two cases of conscience may serve as examples of the vast range of instances of a conflict of loyalties. And now you may ask: What will our principle do to decide such cases?

VII

I reply at once by emphasizing the fact that the precept, *Be loyal to loyalty*, implies two characteristics of loyal conduct which are, to my mind, inseparable. The first characteristic is Decisiveness on the part of the loyal moral agent. The second characteristic is Fidelity to loyal decisions once made, in so far as later insight does not clearly forbid the continuance of such fidelity. Let me indicate what I mean by these two characteristics.

Loyalty to loyalty is never a merely pious wish. It is personal devotion. This devotion shows itself by action, not by mere sentiments. Loyalty to loyalty hence requires the choice of some definite mode of action. And this mode of action involves, in critical cases, some new choice of a personal cause, through which the loyal agent undertakes to serve henceforth, as best he can, the general cause of the loyalty of mankind. Now, my special choice of my personal cause is always fallible. For I can never know with certainty but that, if I were wiser, I should better see my way to serving universal loyalty than I now see it. Thus, if I choose to be loyal to loyalty by becoming a loyal clerk or a watchman or a lighthouse keeper, I can never know but that, in some other calling, I might have done better. Now, it is no part of the precept, *Be loyal to loyalty*, to tell me, or to pretend to tell me, what my most effective vocation is. Doubts about that topic are in so far not moral doubts. They are mere expressions of my general ignorance of the world and of my own powers. If I indeed happen to know that I have no power to make a good clerk or a good watchman, the precept about loyalty then tells me that it would be disloyal to waste my powers in an undertaking for which I am so unfit. If, of various possible ways of undertaking to be loyal to loyalty, my present insight already tells me that one will, in my case, certainly succeed best of all, then, indeed, the general principle of loyalty requires me to have neither eyes to see nor tongue to speak save as this best mode of service commands. But if, at the critical moment, I cannot predict which of two modes of serving the cause of loyalty to loyalty will lead to the more complete success in such service, the general principle certainly cannot tell me which of these two modes of service to choose.

And, nevertheless, the principle does not desert me, even at the moment of my greatest ignorance. It is still my guide. For it now becomes the principle, *Have a cause; choose your cause; be decisive.* In this form the principle is just as practical as it would be if my knowledge of the world and of my own powers were infallible. For it forbids cowardice; it forbids hesitancy beyond the point where further consideration can be reasonably expected, for the present, to throw new light on the situation. It forbids me to play Hamlet's part. It requires me, in a loyal spirit and in the light of all that I now know, to choose and to proceed to action, not as one who believes himself omniscient, but as one who knows that the only way to be loyal is to act loyally, however ignorantly one has to act.

Otherwise stated, the case is this. I hesitate at the critical moment between conflicting causes. For the sake of loyalty to loyalty, which one of two conflicting special causes shall I henceforth undertake to serve? This is my question. If I knew what is to be the outcome, I could at once easily choose. I am ignorant of the outcome. In so far I indeed cannot tell which to choose. But in one respect I am, nevertheless, already committed. I have already undertaken to be loyal to loyalty. In so far, then, I already have my cause. If so, however, I have neither eyes to see nor tongue to speak save as this my highest cause commands. Now, what does this my highest cause, loyalty to loyalty, command? It commands simply but imperatively that, since I must serve, and since, at this critical moment, my only service must take the form of a choice between loyalties, I shall choose, even in my ignorance, what form my service is henceforth to take. The point where I am to make this choice is determined by the obvious fact that, after a certain waiting to find out whatever I can find out, I always reach the moment when further indecision would of itself constitute a sort of decision, — a decision, namely, to do nothing, and so not to serve at all. Such a decision to do nothing, my loyalty to loyalty forbids; and therefore my principle clearly says to me after a fair consideration of the case: *Decide, knowingly if you can, ignorantly if you must, but in any case decide, and have no fear.*

The duty of decisiveness as to one's loyalty is thus founded upon considerations analogous to those which Professor James has emphasized, in speaking of certain problems about belief in his justly famous essay on the Will to Believe. *As soon as further indecision would itself practically amount to a decision to do nothing,* — and so would mean a failure to be loyal to loyalty, — *then at once decide.* This is the only right act. If you cannot decide knowingly, put your own personal will into the matter, and thereupon decide ignorantly. For ignorant service, which still knows itself as a willing attempt to serve the cause of universal loyalty, is better than a knowing refusal to undertake any service whatever. The duty to decide is, in such cases, just that upon which our principle insists.

Decision, however, is meaningless unless it is to be followed up by persistently active loyalty. Having surrendered the self to the chosen special cause, loyalty, precisely as loyalty to loyalty, forbids you to destroy the unity of your own purposes, and to set the model of disloyalty before your fellows, by turning back from the cause once chosen, unless indeed later growth in knowledge makes manifest that further service of that special cause would henceforth involve unquestionable disloyalty to universal loyalty. Fidelity to the cause once chosen is as obvious an aspect of a thorough devotion of the self to the cause of universal loyalty, as is decisiveness.

Only a growth in knowledge which makes it evident that the special cause once chosen is an unworthy cause, disloyal to universal loyalty,— only such a growth in knowledge can absolve from fidelity to the cause once chosen. In brief, the choice of a special personal cause is a sort of ethical marriage to this cause, with the exception that the duty to choose some personal cause is a duty for everybody, while marriage is not everybody's duty. The marriage to your cause is not to be dissolved unless it becomes unquestionably evident that the continuance of this marriage involves positive unfaithfulness to the cause of universal loyalty. But like any other marriage, the marriage of each self to its chosen personal cause is made in ignorance of the consequences. Decide, then, in the critical case, and, "forsaking all others, cleave to your own cause." Thus only can you be loyal to loyalty.

If you once view the matter in this way, you will not suppose that our principle would leave either the future General Lee or our supposed young professional woman without guidance. It would say: Look first at the whole situation. Consider it carefully. See, if possible, whether you can predict the consequences to the general loyalty which your act will involve. If, after such consideration, you still remain ignorant of decisive facts, then look to your highest loyalty; look steadfastly at the cause of universal loyalty itself. Remember how the loyal have always borne themselves. Then, with your eyes and your voice put as completely as may be at the service of that cause, arouse all the loyal interests of your own self, just as they now are, to their fullest vigor; and hereupon firmly and freely decide. Henceforth, with all your mind and soul and strength belong, fearlessly and faithfully, to the chosen personal cause until the issue is decided, or until you positively know that this cause can no longer be served without disloyalty. So act, and you are morally right.

Now, that is how Lee acted. And that, too, is how all the loyal of our own Northern armies acted. And to-day we know how there was indeed loyalty to loyalty upon both sides, and how all those thus loyal actually served the one cause of the now united nation. They loyally shed their blood, North and South, that we might be free from their burden of hatred and of horror. Precisely so should the young woman of our ideal instance choose. It is utterly vain for another to tell her which she ought to choose, — her profession or her family. But it would be equally vain, and an insult to loyalty, lightly to say to her: Do as you please. One can say to her: Either of these lives, — the life of the successful servant of a profession, or the life of the devoted sister or aunt, — either, if loyally lived, is indeed a whole life. Nobody ought to ask for a more blessed lot than is either of these lives, — however obscure the household drudgery of the one may be, however hard beset by cares the worldly success of the other may prove, or however toilsome either of them in prospect is, so long as either is faithfully lived out in full devotion. For nobody has anything better than loyalty, or can get anything better. But one of them alone can you live. No mortal knows which is the better for your world. With all your heart, in the name of universal loyalty, choose. And then be faithful to the choice. So shall it be morally well with you.

Now, if this view of the application of our precept is right, you see how our principle is just to that mysterious and personal aspect of conscience upon which common sense insists. Such a loyal choice as I have described demands, of course, one's will, — one's conscious decisiveness. It also calls out all of one's personal and more or less unconsciously present instincts, interests, affections, one's socially formed habits, and whatever else is woven into the unity of each individual self. Loyalty, as we have all along seen, is a willing devotion. Since it is willing, it involves conscious choice. Since it is devotion, it involves all the mystery of finding out that some cause awakens us, fascinates us, reverberates through our whole being, possesses us. It is a fact that critical decisions as to the direction of our loyalty can be determined by our own choice. It is also a fact that loyalty involves more than mere conscious choice. It involves that response of our entire nature, conscious and unconscious, which makes loyalty so precious. Now, this response of the whole nature of the self, when the result is a moral decision, is what common sense has in mind when it views our moral decisions as due to our conscience, but our conscience as a mysterious higher or deeper self.

As a fact, the conscience is the ideal of the self, coming to consciousness as a present command. It says, *Be loyal.* If one asks, *Loyal to what?* the conscience, awakened by our whole personal response to the need of mankind replies, *Be loyal to loyalty.* If, hereupon, various loyalties seem to conflict, the conscience says: *Decide.* If one asks, *How decide?* conscience further urges, *Decide as I, your conscience, the ideal expression of your whole personal nature, conscious and unconscious, find best.* If one persists, *But you and I may be wrong,* the last word of conscience is, *We are fallible, but we can be decisive and faithful; and this is loyalty.*

V

SOME AMERICAN PROBLEMS IN THEIR RELATION TO LOYALTY

LECTURE V

SOME AMERICAN PROBLEMS IN THEIR RELATION TO LOYALTY

IN the philosophy of loyalty, whose general statement has been contained in the foregoing lectures, I have made an effort to reconcile the conception of loyalty with that of a rational and moral individualism. To every ethical individualist I have said: In loyalty alone is the fulfilment of the reasonable purposes of your individualism. If you want true freedom, seek it in loyalty. If you want self-expression, spirituality, moral autonomy, loyalty alone can give you these goods. But equally I have insisted upon interpreting loyalty in terms that emphasize the significance of the individual choice of that personal cause to which one is to be loyal. This evening, as I approach the application of our philosophy of loyalty to some well-known American problems, it is important for us to bear in mind from the outset this synthesis of individualism and loyalty which constitutes our whole ethical doctrine.

I

The traditional view of loyalty has associated the term, in the minds of most of you, with moral situations in which some external social power predetermines for the individual, without his consent, all the causes to which he ought to be loyal. Loyalty so conceived appears to be opposed to individual liberty. But in our philosophy of loyalty there is only one cause which is rationally and absolutely determined for the individual as the right cause for him as for everybody,—this is the general cause defined by the phrase *loyalty to loyalty*. The way in which any one man is to show his loyalty to loyalty is, however, in our philosophy of loyalty, something which varies endlessly with the individual, and which can never be precisely defined except by and through his personal consent. I can be loyal to loyalty only in my own fashion, and by serving my own special personal system of causes. How wide a range of moral freedom of conscience this fact gives me, we began at the last time to see. In order to make that fact still clearer, let me sum up our moral code afresh, and in another order than the one used at the last time.

As our philosophy of loyalty states the case, the moral law is: (1) be loyal; (2) to that end have a special cause or a system of causes which shall constitute your personal object of loyalty, your business in life; (3) choose this cause, in the first place, for yourself, but decisively, and so far as the general principle of loyalty permits, remain faithful to this chosen cause, until the work that you can do for it is done; and (4) the general principle of loyalty to which all special choices of one's cause are subject, is the principle: Be loyal to loyalty, that is, do what you can to produce a maximum of the devoted service of causes, a maximum of fidelity, and of selves that choose and serve fitting objects of loyalty.

From the point of view of this statement of the moral law, we are all in the wrong in case we have no cause whatever to which we are loyal. If you are an individualist in the sense that you are loyal to nothing, you are certainly false to your duty. Furthermore, in order that you should be loyal at all, the cause to which you are loyal must involve the union of various persons by means of some social tie, which has in some respects an impersonal or superindividual character, as well as a distinct personal interest for each of the persons concerned.

On the other hand, my statement of the moral principle gives to us all an extremely limited right to judge what the causes are to which any one of our neighbors ought to devote himself. Having defined loyalty as I have done as a devotion to a cause, outside the private self, and yet chosen by this individual self as his cause; having pointed out the general nature which such a cause must possess in order to be worthy,—namely, having shown that it must involve the mentioned union of

202

personal and impersonal interests; having, furthermore, asserted that all rightly chosen loyalty is guided by the intent not to enter into any unnecessary destruction of the loyalty of others, but is inspired by loyalty to loyalty, and so seeks, as best the loyal individual can, to further loyalty as a common good for all mankind,—having said so much, I must, from my point of view, leave to the individual the decision as to the choice of the cause or causes to which he is loyal, subject only to these mentioned conditions. I have very little right to judge, except by the most unmistakable expression of my fellow's purpose, whether he is actually loyal, in the sense of my definition, or not.

I may say of a given person that I do not understand to what cause he is loyal. But I can assert that he is disloyal only when I know what cause it is to which he has committed himself, and what it is that he has done to be false to his chosen fidelity. Or again, I can judge that he lacks loyalty if he makes it perfectly evident by his acts or by his own confessions that he has chosen no cause at all. If he is unquestionably loyal to something, to his country or to his profession or to his family, I may criticise his expression of loyalty, in so far as I clearly see that it involves him in unnecessary assault upon the loyalty of others, or upon their means to be loyal. Thus, all unnecessary personal aggression upon what we commonly call the rights of other individuals are excluded by my formula, simply because in case I deprive my fellow of his property, his life, or his physical integrity, I take away from him the only means whereby he can express in a practical way whatever loyalty he has.) Hence such aggression, unless necessary, involves disloyalty to the general loyalty of mankind, is a crime against humanity at large, and is inconsistent with any form of loyalty. Such is the range of judgment that we have a right to use in our moral estimates of other people. The range thus indicated is, as I have insisted, large enough to enable us to define all rationally defensible special principles regarding right and wrong acts. Murder, lying, evil speaking, unkindness, are from this point of view simply forms of disloyalty.

But my right to judge the choices of my fellow is thus very sharply limited. I cannot say that he is disloyal because his personal cause is not my cause, or because I have no sympathy with the objects to which he devotes himself. I have no right to call him disloyal because I should find that if I were to do what he does, I should indeed be disloyal to causes that I accept. I may not judge a man to be without an object of loyalty merely because I do not understand what the object is with which he busies himself. I may regard his cause as too narrow, if I clearly see that he could do better service than he does to the cause of universal loyalty. But when I observe how much even the plainest and humblest of the loyal sometimes unconsciously do to help others to profit by the contagion of their own loyalty, by the example of their faithfulness, I must be cautious about judging another man's cause to be too narrow. You cannot easily set limits to the occupations that the sincere choice of somebody will make expressions of genuine loyalty. The loyal individual may live largely alone; or mainly in company. His life may be spent in the office or in the study or in the workshop or in the field; in arctic exploration, in philanthropy, in a laboratory. And yet the true form and spirit of loyalty, and of loyalty to loyalty, when once you get an actual understanding of the purposes of the self that is in question, is universal and unmistakable.

I hesitate, therefore, to decide for another person even such a question as the way in which his most natural and obvious opportunities for loyalty shall be used. It is true that nature furnishes to us all opportunities for loyalty which it seems absurd to neglect. Charity, as they say, begins at home. Still more obviously does loyalty naturally begin at home. People who wholly neglect their natural family ties often thereby make probable that they are disloyal people. Yet the well-known word about hating father and mother in the service of a universal cause paradoxically states a possibility to which the history of the early Christian martyrs more than once gave an actual embodiment. If the martyr might break loose from all family ties in his loyal service of his faith, one cannot attempt to determine for another person at just what point the neglect of a naturally present opportunity for loyalty becomes an inevitable incident of the choice of loyalty that one has made. Nature, after all, furnishes us merely our opportunities to be loyal. Some of these must be used. None of them may be so ignored that thereby we deliberately increase the disloyalty of mankind. But the individual retains the inalienable duty, which nobody, not even his most pious critical neighbor, can either perform or wholly judge for him, — the duty to decide wherein his own loyalty lies. Yet the duty to be loyal to loyalty is absolutely universal and rigid.

As we also saw at the last time, since fidelity and loyalty are indeed inseparable, the breaking of the once plighted faith is always a disloyal act, unless the discovery that the original undertaking involves one in disloyalty to the general cause of loyalty requires the change. Thus, indeed, the once awakened and so far loyal member of the robber band would be bound by his newly discovered loyalty to humanity in general, to break his oath to the band. But even in such a case, he would still owe to his comrades of the former service a kind of fidelity which he would not have owed had he never been a member of the band. His duty to his former comrades would change through his new insight. But he could never ignore his former loyalty, and would never be absolved from the peculiar obligation to his former comrades,—the obligation to help them all to a higher service of humanity than they had so far attained.

You see, from this point of view, how the requirements of the spirit of loyalty are in one sense perfectly stern and unyielding, while in another sense they are and must be capable of great freedom of interpretation. In judging myself, in deciding how I can best be loyal to loyalty, in deciding what special causes they are through which I am to express my loyalty, in judging whether my act is justified by my loyalty, — in all these respects I must be with myself, at least in principle, entirely rigid. As I grow in knowledge, I shall better learn how to be loyal. I shall learn to serve new causes, to recover from vain attempts at a service of which I was incapable, and in general to become a better servant of the cause. But at each point of my choice my obligation to be loyal, to have a cause, to have for the purposes of voluntary conduct no eyes and ears and voice save as this cause directs, — this obligation is absolute. I cannot excuse myself from it without being false to my own purpose. I may sleep or be slothful, but precisely in so far as such relaxation fits me for work. I may amuse myself, but because amusement is again a necessary preliminary to or accompaniment of loyal service. I may seek my private advantage, but only in so far as, since I am an instrument of my cause, it is indeed my duty, and is consistent with my loyalty, to furnish to the cause an effective instrument. But the general principle remains: Working or idle, asleep or awake, joyous or sorrowful, thoughtful or apparently careless, at critical moments, or when engaged in the most mechanical routine, in so far as my will can determine what I am, I must be whatever my loyalty requires me to be. And in so far my voluntary life is from my point of view a topic for judgments which are in principle perfectly determinate.

Profoundly different must be my judgment in case of my estimate of the loyalty of my fellow. The tasks of mankind are not only common but also individual. So long as you are sure of your own loyalty, and do not break your trust, I cannot judge that you are actually disloyal. I can only judge in some respects whether your loyalty is or is not enlightened, is or is not successful, is or is not in unnecessary conflict with the loyalty of others. I have to be extremely wary of deciding what the loyalty of others demands of them. But this I certainly know, that if a man has made no choice for himself of the cause that he serves, he is not yet come to his rational self, he has not yet found his business as a moral agent.

II

Such are our general results regarding the nature of loyalty as an ethical principle. This complete synthesis of loyalty with a rational individualism must be borne in mind as we attempt a certain practical application of these principles to the problem of our present American life. If there is any truth in the foregoing, then our concept especially helps us in trying to define what it is that we most need in the social life of a democracy, and what means we have of doing something to satisfy the moral needs of our American community, while leaving the liberties of the people intact.

Liberty without loyalty — of what worth, if the foregoing principles are sound, could such liberty be to any people? And yet, if you recall the protest of my young friend, the Russian immigrant's son, as cited to you in a former lecture, you will be reminded of the great task that now lies before our American people,

—the task of teaching millions of foreign birth and descent to understand and to bear constantly in mind the value of loyalty, the task also of keeping our own loyalty intact in the presence of those enormous complications of social life which the vastness of our country, and the numbers of our foreign immigrants are constantly increasing. The problem here in question is not merely the problem of giving instruction in the duties of citizenship to those to whom our country is new, nor yet of awakening and preserving patriotism. It is the problem of keeping alive what we now know to be the central principle of the moral life in a population which is constantly being altered by new arrivals, and unsettled by great social changes.

If you recall what was said in our former lecture regarding modern individualism in general, you will also see that our American immigration problem is only one aspect of a world-wide need of moral enlightenment, — a need characteristic of our time. One is tempted to adapt Lincoln's great words, and to say that in all nations, but particularly in America, we need in this day to work together to the end that loyalty of the people, by the people, and for the people shall not perish from the earth.

It is not, indeed, that loyal people no longer are frequent amongst us. The faithful who live and die in loyalty so far as they know loyalty are indeed not yet uncommon. The loyalty of the common people is precisely the most precious moral treasure of our world. But the moral dangers of our American civilization are twofold. First, loyalty is not sufficiently prominent amongst our explicit social ideals in America. It is too much left to the true-hearted obscure people. It is not sufficiently emphasized. Our popular literature too often ignores it or misrepresents it. This is one danger, since it means that loyalty is too often discouraged and confused, instead of glorified and honored. In the long run, if not checked, this tendency must lead to a great decrease of loyalty. The second danger lies in the fact that when loyalty is indeed emphasized and glorified, it is then far too seldom conceived as rationally involving loyalty to universal loyalty. Hence we all think too often of loyalty as a warlike and intolerant virtue, and not as the spirit of universal peace. Enlightened loyalty, as we have now learned, means harm to no man's loyalty. It is at war only with disloyalty, and its warfare, unless necessity constrains, is only a spiritual warfare. It does not foster class hatreds; it knows of nothing reasonable about race prejudices, and it regards all races of men as one in their need of loyalty. It ignores mutual misunderstandings. It loves its own wherever upon earth its own, namely, loyalty itself, is to be found. Enlightened loyalty takes no delight in great armies or in great navies for their own sake. If it consents to them, it views them merely as transiently necessary calamities. It has no joy in national prowess, except in so far as that prowess means a furtherance of universal loyalty. And it regards the war-spirit, which in our first lecture we used as an example of loyalty,—it regards this spirit, I say, as at its best an outcome of necessity or else of unenlightened loyalty, and as at its worst one of the basest of disloyalties to universal loyalty.

Now, it is precisely this enlightened form of loyalty, this conception of loyalty to loyalty, which we most need to have taught to our American people, — taught openly, explicitly, — yet not taught, for the most part, by the now too familiar method of fascinating denunciations of the wicked, nor by the mere display of force, social or political, nor by the setting of class against class, nor yet by any glorification of mere power, nor by appeals merely to patriotic but confused fervor. We want loyalty to loyalty taught by helping many people to be loyal to their own special causes, and by showing them that loyalty is a precious common human good, and that it can never be a good to harm any man's loyalty except solely in necessary defence of our own loyalty.

III

From the point of view of the foregoing discussion, if you want to do the best you can to teach loyalty, not now to single individuals, but to great masses of people, — masses such as our whole nation, — you should do three things: (1) You should aid them to possess and to keep those physical and mental powers and possessions which are the necessary conditions for the exercise of loyalty. (2) You should provide them with manifold opportunities to be loyal, that is, with a maximum of significant, rational enterprises, such as can be loyally carried out; you should, if possible, secure for them a minimum of the conditions that lead to the conflicts of various forms of loyalty; and you should furnish them a variety of opportunities to get social experience of the value of loyalty. (3) You should explicitly show them that loyalty is the best of human goods, and that loyalty to loyalty is the crown and the real meaning of all loyalty.

Helping the people to the attainment and preservation of their powers obviously involves the sort of care of public health, the sort of general training of intelligence, the sort of protection and assistance, which our philan-

thropists and teachers and public-spirited people generally regard as important. There is
no doubt that in our modern American life our
social order does give to great numbers of
people care and assistance and protection,
such as earlier stages of civilization lacked.
But the other side of the task of providing
our people with the means of ethical advance-
ment, the side that has to do with letting them
know what loyalty is, and with giving them
opportunities to be loyal, this side, I say, of
what we ought to do to further the moral prog-
ress of our people, is at present very imperfectly accomplished.

With prosperity, as we may well admit, sympathy, benevolence, public spirit, even the
more rational philanthropy which seeks not
merely to relieve suffering, but to improve the
effective powers of those whom we try to help,
— all these things have become, in recent
decades, more and more prominent on the
better side of our civilization. And yet I
insist, just as prosperity is not virtue, and just
as power is not morality, so too even public

charity, and even the disposition to train people, to make them more intelligent, to give
them new power, all such dispositions are insufficient to insure the right moral training of
our people, or the effective furtherance of ideal
life amongst them.

What men need involves opportunity for
loyalty. And such opportunity they get, especially through the suggestion of objects to
which they can be loyal. If you want to train
a man to a good life, you must indeed do what
you can to give him health and power. And
you do something for him when, by example
and by precept, you encourage him to be sympathetic, public-spirited, amiable, or industri-
ous. But benevolence; sympathy, what some
people love to call altruism, —these are all mere
fragments of goodness, mere aspects of the
dutiful life. What is needed is loyalty. Meanwhile, since loyalty is so plastic a virtue, since
the choice of the objects of loyalty must vary so
widely from individual to individual, and since,
above all, you can never force anybody to be
loyal, but can only show him opportunities

for loyalty, and teach him by example and precept what loyalty is, the great need of any higher civilization is a vast variety of opportunities for individual loyalty, and of suggestion regarding what forms of loyalty are possible.

Now, I need not for a moment ignore the fact that every higher civilization, and of course our own, presents to any intelligent person numerous opportunities to be loyal. But what I must point out in our present American life is, that our opportunities for loyalty are not rightly brought to our consciousness by the conditions of our civilization, so that a great mass of our people are far too little reminded of what chances for loyalty they themselves have, or of what loyalty is. Meanwhile our national prosperity and our national greatness involve us all in many new temptations to disloyalty, and distract our minds too much from dwelling upon the loyal side of life; so that at the very moment when our philanthropy is growing, when our sympathies are constantly aroused through the press, the drama, and our sensitive social life generally, our training in loyalty is falling away. Our young people grow up with a great deal of their attention fixed upon personal success, and also with a great deal of training in sympathetic sentiments; but they get far too little knowledge, either practical or theoretical, of what loyalty means.

IV

The first natural opportunity for loyalty is furnished by family ties. We all know how some of the conditions of our civilization tend with great masses of our population to a new interpretation of family ties in which family loyalty often plays a much less part than it formerly did in family life. Since our modern family is less patriarchal than it used to be, our children, trained in an individualistic spirit, frequently make little of certain duties to their parents which the ancient family regarded as imperative and exalted as ideal. Many of us deliberately prefer the loss of certain results of the patriarchal family tie, and are glad that in the modern American family the parental decisions regarding the marriage choices of children are so much less decisive than they used to be. Many insist that other weakenings of the family tie, such as divorce legislation and the practice of divorce have involved, are in the direction of a reasonable recognition of individual interests.

I will not try to discuss these matters at length. But this I can say without hesitation: The family ties, so far as they are natural, are opportunities for loyalty; so far as they are deliberately chosen or recognized, are instances of the choice of a loyalty. From our point of view, therefore, they must be judged as all other opportunities and forms of loyalty are judged. That such opportunities and forms alter their character as civilization changes is inevitable, and need be no matter for superstitious cares regarding whatever was arbitrary in traditional views of family authority. But, after all, fidelity and family devotion are amongst the most precious opportunities and instances of loyalty. Faithlessness can never become a virtue, however your traditions about the forms of faithfulness may vary in their external details. Whoever deliberately breaks the tie to which he is devoted loses the opportunity and the position of the loyal self, and in so far loses the best sort of thing that there is in the moral world. No fondness for individualism will ever do away with this fact. We want more individuals and more rational individualism; but the only possible ethical use of an individual is to be loyal. He has no other destiny.

When a man feels his present ties to be arbitrary or to be a mechanical bondage, he sometimes says that it is irrational to be a mere spoke in a wheel. Now, a loyal self is always more than a spoke in a wheel. But still, at the worst, it is better to be a spoke in the wheel than a spoke out of the wheel. And you never make ethical individuals, or enlarge their opportunities, merely by breaking ties. Hence, so far as a change in family tradition actually involves a loss of opportunities and forms of loyalty, which tradition used to emphasize, our new social order has lost a good thing. Do we see at present just what is taking its place? If the patriarchal family must pass away or be profoundly altered, surely we should not gain thereby unless there were to result a new family type, as rich in appeal to our human affections and our domestic instincts as the old forms ever were.

But in our present American life the family tie has been weakened, and yet no substitute has been found. We have so far lost certain opportunities for loyalty.

Now, how shall we hope to win back these opportunities? I answer: We can win back something of what we have lost if only we in this country can get before ourselves and our public a new, a transformed conception of what loyalty is. The loyalties of the past have lost their meaning for many people, simply because people have confounded loyalty with mere bondage to tradition, or with mere surrender of individual rights and preferences. Such people have forgotten that what has made loyalty a good has never been the convention which undertook to enforce it, but has always been the spiritual dignity which lies in being loyal.

As to individual rights and preferences, nobody can ever attain either the one or the other, in full measure, apart from loyalty to the closest and the most lasting ties which the life of the individual in question is capable of accepting with hearty willingness. Ties once loyally accepted may be broken in case, but only in case, the further keeping of those ties intact involves disloyalty to the universal cause of loyalty. When such reason for breaking ties exists, to break them becomes a duty; and then, indeed, a merely conventional persistence in what has become a false position, is itself a disloyal deed. But ties may never be broken except for the sake of other and still stronger ties. No one may rationally say: "Loyalty can no longer bind me, because, from my deepest soul, I feel that I want my individual freedom." For any such outcry comes from an ignorance of what one's deepest soul really wants.

Disloyalty is moral suicide. Many a poor human creature outlives all that, in the present life, can constitute his true self, — outlives as a mere psychological specimen any human expression of his moral personality, and does so because he has failed to observe that his loyalty, so far and so long as it has been his own, has been the very heart of this moral personality. When loyalty has once been fully aroused, and has then not merely blundered but died, there may, indeed, remain much fluttering eagerness of life; as if a stranded ship's torn canvas were still flapping in the wind. But there cannot remain freedom of personal existence. For the moral personality that once was loyal, and that then blindly sought freedom, is, to human vision, dead. What is, in such a case, left of the so-called life is merely an obituary. Curious people of prominence have sometimes expressed a wish to read their own obituaries. But it is hardly worth while to live them.

People sometimes fail to observe this fact, partly because they conceive loyalty as something which convention forces upon the individual, and partly because they also conceive loyalty, where it exists, as merely a relation of one individual to other individuals. Both views, as we now know, are wrong. No convention can predetermine my personal loyalty without my free consent. But then, if I loyally consent, I mean to be faithful; I give myself; I am henceforth the self thus given over to the cause; and therefore essential unfaithfulness is, for me, moral suicide. Meanwhile, however, no mere individual can ever be my whole object of loyalty; for to another individual human being I can only say, "So far as in me lies I will be loyal to *our* tie, to *our* cause, to *our union*." For this reason the loyal are never the mere slaves of convention; and, on the other hand, they can never say one to another, "Since we have now grown more or less tired of one another, our loyalty ceases." To tire of the cause to which my whole self is once for all committed, is indeed to tire of being my moral self. I cannot win my freedom in that way. And no individual, as individual, ever has been, or ever can be, my whole cause. My cause has always been a tie, an union of various individuals in one.

Now, can our American people learn this lesson in so far as this lesson is illustrated by family ties? Can they come to see that loyalty does not mean the bondage of one individual to another, but does mean the exaltation of individuals to the rank of true personalities by virtue of their free acceptance of enduring causes, and by virtue of their lifelong service of their common personal ties? If this lesson can be learned by those serious-minded people who have been misled, in recent times, by a false form of individualism, then we shall indeed not get rid of our moral problems, but we shall vastly simplify our moral situation. And a rational individualism will still remain our possession. How to treat the disloyal remains indeed a serious practical problem. But we shall never learn to deal with that problem if we suppose that the one cure for disloyalty, or the one revenge which we can take upon the disloyal, lies in a new act of disloyalty, that is, in the mere assertion of our individual freedom. Train our people to know the essential preciousness of loyalty. In that way only can you hope to restore to the family, not, indeed, all of its older conventional forms, but its true dignity. The problem, then, of the salvation of the family life of our nation resolves itself into the general problem of how to train our people at large into loyalty to loyalty.

V

The second great opportunity for loyalty is furnished, to the great mass of our people, by their relations to our various political powers and institutions, and to our larger social organizations generally. And here we meet, in the America of to-day, with many signs that our political and social life form at present a poor school in the arts of loyalty to loyalty.

Loyalty, indeed, as I have repeatedly said, we still have present all about us. The precious plain and obscure people, who are loyal to whatever they understand to be worthy

causes, and, on the other hand, those prominent and voluntary public servants, who in so
many cases are our leaders in good works, —
these we have so far still with us. And new
forms of loyalty constantly appear in our social life. Reform movements, trades-unions,
religious sects, partisan organizations, both good
and evil, arouse in various ways the loyalty of
great numbers of people. Yet these special
loyalties do not get rightly organized in such
form as to further loyalty to loyalty. Narrow
loyalties, side by side with irrational forms
of individualism and with a cynical contempt
for all loyalty, — these are what we too often
see in the life of our country. For where the
special loyalties are, amongst our people, most
developed, they far too often take the form of
a loyalty to mutually hostile partisan organizations, or to sects, or to social classes, at the
expense of loyalty to the community or to the
whole country. The labor-unions demand and
cultivate the loyalty of their members; but
they do so with a far too frequent emphasis
upon the thesis that in order to be loyal to his

own social class, or, in particular, to his union, the laborer must disregard certain duties to the community at large, and to the nation, — duties which loyalty to loyalty seems obviously to require. And party loyalty comes to be misused by corrupt politicians to the harm of the state. Therefore loyalty to special organizations such as labor-unions comes to be misdirected by such leaders as are disloyal, until the welfare of the whole social order is endangered.

The result is that the very spirit of loyalty itself has come to be regarded with suspicion by many of our social critics, and by many such partisans of ethical individualism as those whose various views we studied in our second lecture. Yet surely if such ethical individualists, objecting to the mischiefs wrought by the corrupt politicians, or by the more unwise leaders of organized labor, imagine that loyalty is responsible for these evils, such critics have only to turn to the recent history of corporate misdeeds and of the unwise mismanagement of corporations in this country, in order to be reminded that what we want, at present, from some of the managers of great corporate interests is more loyalty, and less of the individualism of those who seek power. And I myself should say that precisely the same sort of loyalty is what we want both from the leaders and from the followers of organized labor. There is here one law for all.

Meanwhile, in case of the ill-advised labor agitations, and of the corrupt party management, the cure, if it ever comes, surely will include cultivating amongst our people the spirit of loyalty to loyalty. Loyalty in itself is never an evil. The arbitrary interference with other men's loyalties, the disloyalty to the universal cause of loyalty, is what does the mischief here in question. The more the laborer is loyal to his union, if only he learns to conceive this loyalty as an instance of loyalty to loyalty, the more likely is his union to become, in the end, an instrument for social harmony, and not, as is now too often the case, an influence for oppression and for social disorganization. The loyalty which the trades-unions demand of their members is at present too often viewed as a mere class loyalty, and also as opposed to the individual freedom of choice on the part of those laborers who do not belong to a given union, or even to those who are in the union, but whose right choice and interests are sometimes hindered by their own union itself. But our people must learn that loyalty does not mean hostility to another man's loyalty. Loyalty is for all men, kings and laborers alike; and whenever we learn to recognize that fact, loyalty will no longer mean fraternal strife, and will no longer excuse treason to the country for the sake of fidelity to corrupt leaders or to mischievous agitations.

VI

But you may hereupon ask how the masses of our people are to learn such a lesson of loyalty to loyalty. I admit that the problem of teaching our people what the larger loyalty means is at present peculiarly difficult. And it is rendered all the more difficult by the fact that, for us Americans, loyalty to our nation, as a whole, is a sentiment that we find to be at present by no means as prominent in the minds of our people as such sentiments have been in the past in other nations. Let me explain what I mean by this assertion.

The history of our sentiment towards our national government is somewhat different from the history of the sentiment of patriotism in other countries. We have never had a king as the symbol of our national dignity and unity. We have, on the other hand, never had to war against a privileged class. Our constitutional problem which led to the Civil War was a different problem from that which the French Revolution, or the English political wars of the seventeenth century, have exemplified. At one time loyalty to the nation stood, in the minds of many of our people, in strong contrast to their loyalty to their state, or to their section of the country. This contrast led in many cases to a bitter conflict between the two sorts of loyal interests. At last such conflicts had to be decided by war. The result of the war was such that, from one point of view, the national government and the authority of the nation, as a whole, have won a position that is at present politically unquestionable. The supremacy of the national government in its own sphere is well recognized. Within its legal limits, its power is popularly regarded as irresistible. The appearance of its soldiers at any moment of popular tumult is well known to be the most effective expression of public authority which we have at our disposal, even although the body of soldiers which may be accessible for such a show of force happens to be a very small body. Viewed, then, as a legal authority and as a physical force, our national government occupies at present a peculiarly secure position. And so, the President of the United States is, at any moment, more powerful than almost any living monarch. All this, viewed as the outcome of our long constitutional struggle, would seem of itself to suggest that the American people have become essentially loyal to our national government.

But, nevertheless, is this quite true? I

think that almost any thoughtful American has to admit that in time of peace we do not regard our national government with any such intense sentiments of loyalty as would seem from report to be the living, the vital, the constant possession of Japanese patriots when they consider their traditional devotion to the nation and to their emperor. For them their country is part of a religion. In their consciousness it is said especially to be the land sacred to the memory of their dead. The living, as they say, are but of to-day. The dead they have always with them in memory, even if not in the determinate form of any fixed belief with regard to the precise nature of the life beyond the grave. It is said that the Japanese are very free as to the formulation of all their religious opinions. But in any case their religion includes a reverence for the historic past, a devotion to the dead whose memory makes their country sacred, and a present loyalty which is consciously determined by these religious motives.

Now, the most patriotic American can hardly

pretend that he consciously views his country, taken as a whole, in any such religious way. The country is to us an unquestionable political authority. Were it in danger, we should rally to its defence. We have a good many formal phrases of reverence for its history and for its dignity,—phrases which had a much more concrete meaning for our predecessors, when the country was smaller, or when the country was in greater danger from its foes. But, at present, is not our national loyalty somewhat in the background of our practical consciousness? Are we really at present a highly patriotic people? Certainly, the observer of a presidential canvass can hardly think of that canvass as a religious function, or believe that a profound reverence for the sacred memory of the fathers is at present a very prominent factor in determining our choice of the party for which we shall vote at the polls.

And if you say that political dissensions are always of such a nature as to hide for the moment patriotism behind a mist of present perplexities, you may well be asked in reply whether anywhere else, outside of political dissensions, we have in our national life functions, ceremonies, expressions of practical devotion to our nation as an ideal, which serve to keep our loyalty to our country sufficiently alive, and sufficiently a factor in our lives. When can the ordinary American citizen say in time of peace that he performs notable acts of devotion to his country, such that he could describe those acts in the terms that the Speaker of the House of Commons used, in the story that I reported to you in my former lecture? In other words, how often, in your own present life, or in the lives of your fellow-citizens, as now you know them, is it the case that you do something critical, significant, involving personal risk or sacrifice to yourself, and something which is meanwhile so inspired by your love of your nation as a whole that you can say that just then you have neither eyes to see nor tongue to speak save as the country itself, in your opinion, requires you to see and to speak?

Now, all this state of things is opposed to

our easily forming a conception of what loyalty to loyalty demands of us in our social and political relations. But the faults in question are not peculiar to our American people. They seem to my mind to be merely symptomatic of something which naturally belongs to the general type of civilization upon which, in our national history, we are entering. The philosopher Hegel, in one of his works on the philosophy of history, depicts a type of civilization, which, in his mind, was especially associated with the decline and fall of the Roman Empire, as well as with the political absolutism of the seventeenth and of the early eighteenth centuries in modern Europe. This type itself was conceived by him as a general one, such that it might be realized in very various ages and civilizations. Hegel called this type of social consciousness the type of the social mind, or of the "Spirit," that had become, as he said, "estranged from itself." Let me explain what Hegel meant by this phrase.

A social consciousness can be of the provincial type; that is, of the type which belongs to small commonwealths or to provinces, such as our own thirteen colonies once were. Or, on the other hand, the social life can be that of the great nation, which is so vast that the individuals concerned no longer recognize their social unity in ways which seem to them homelike. In the province the social mind is naturally aware of itself as at home with its own. In the Roman Empire, or in the state of Louis XIV, nobody is at home. The government in such vast social orders represents the law, a dictation that the individual finds relatively strange to himself. Or, again, the power of the state, even when it is attractive to the individual, still seems to him like a great nature force, rather than like his own loyal self, writ large. The world of the "self-estranged social mind" of Hegel's definition we might, to use a current phraseology, characterize as the world of the imperialistic sort of national consciousness, or simply as the world of imperialism. In such a world, as Hegel skilfully points out, the

individual comes to regard himself as in relation to the social powers, which, in the first
place, he cannot understand. The fact that,
as in our present civilization, he is formally a
free citizen, does not remove his character of
self-estrangement from the social world in
which he moves. Furthermore, since such
a society is so vast as to be no longer easily
intelligible, not only its political, but also its
other social powers, appear to the individual
in a similarly estranged and arbitrary fashion.
In Hegel's account stress is laid upon the inevitable conflicts between wealth and govern-
mental authority, between corporate and political dignities, — conflicts which characterize
the imperial stage of civilization in question.
In the world of the "self-estranged social
mind," loyalty passes into the background,
or tends to disappear altogether. The individual seeks his own. He submits to major
force. Perhaps he finds such submission
welcome, if it secures him safety in the acqui-
sition of private gain, or of stately social position. But welcome or unwelcome, the author-

ity to which he submits, be it the authority of the government or the authority which wealth and the great aggregations of capital imply, is for him just the fact, not a matter for loyalty.

Such a formula as the one which Hegel suggests is always inadequate to the wealth of life. But we are able to understand our national position better when we see that our nation has entered in these days into the realm of the "self-estranged spirit," into the social realm where the distant and irresistible national government, however welcome its authority may be, is at best rather a guarantee of safety, an object for political contest, and a force with which everybody must reckon, than the opportunity for such loyalty, as our distinctly provincial fathers used to feel and express in their early utterances of the national spirit. In the same way in this world of the self-estranged spirit, the other forces of society arouse our curiosity, interest us intensely, must be reckoned with, and may be used more or less wisely to our advantage. But they are the great industrial forces, the aggregations of capital, the combinations of enormous physical power, employed for various social ends. These vast social forces are like the forces of nature. They excite our loyalty as little as do the trade-winds or the blizzard. They leave our patriotic sentiments cold. The smoke of our civilization hides the very heavens that used to be so near, and the stars to which we were once loyal. The consequences of such social conditions are in part inevitable. I am not planning any social reform which would wholly do away with these conditions of the world of the self-estranged spirit. But these conditions of our national social order do not make loyalty to loyalty a less significant need. They only deprive us of certain formerly accessible opportunities for such loyalty. They lead us to take refuge in our unpatriotic sects, partisan organizations, and unions. But they make it necessary that we should try to see how, under conditions as they are, we can best foster loyalty in its higher forms, not by destroying the sects or the unions, but by inspiring them with a new loyalty to loyalty.

As the nation has in so many respects become estranged from our more intimate consciousness, we have lost a portion of what, in the days before the war, used to absorb the loyalty of a large proportion of our countrymen. I speak here of loyalty to the separate states and to the various provinces of our country. Such provincial loyalty still exists, but it has no longer the power that it possessed when it was able to bring on civil war, and very nearly to destroy the national unity. Instead of dangerous sectionalism, we now have the other dangerous tendency towards a war of classes, which the labor-unions and many other symptoms of social discontent emphasize. We have that corrupt political life which partisan mismanagement exemplifies. And we have that total indifference to all forms of loyalty which our seekers after individual power sometimes exhibit, and which occasionally appears as so serious an evil in the conduct of the business of certain great corporations.

All these, I insist, are in our present American life symptoms of the state of the self-estranged spirit. The decline of family loyalty, of which I spoke a while since, may be regarded as another symptom of the same general tendency. Loyalty itself, under such conditions, remains too often unconscious of its true office. Instead of developing into the true loyalty to loyalty, it fails to recognize its own in the vast world of national affairs. It is dazzled by the show of power. It limits its devotion to the service of the political party, or of the labor-union, or of some other sectarian social organization. In private life, as we have seen, it too often loses control of the family. In public life it appears either as the service of a faction, or as a vague fondness for the remote ideals.

VII

And nevertheless, as I insist, loyalty to loyalty is not a vague ideal. The spirit of loyalty is practical, is simple, is teachable, and is for all normal men. And in order to train loyalty to loyalty in a great mass of the people, what is most of all needed is *to help them to be less estranged than they are from their own social order.*

To sum up, then, this too lengthy review, the problem of the training of our American people as a whole to a larger and richer social loyalty is *the problem of educating the self-estranged spirit of our nation to know itself better.* And now that we have the problem before us, what solution can we offer?

The question of what methods a training for loyalty should follow, is the special problem of our next lecture. But there is indeed one proposal, looking towards a better training of our nation to loyalty, which I have here to make as I close this statement of our national needs. The proposal is this. We need and we are beginning to get, in this country, a new and wiser provincialism. I mean by such provincialism no mere renewal of the old sectionalism. I mean the sort of provincialism which makes people want to idealize, to adorn, to ennoble, to educate, their own province; to hold sacred its traditions, to honor its worthy dead, to support and to multiply·its public possessions. I mean the spirit which shows itself in the multiplying of public libraries, in the laying out of public parks, in the work of local historical associations, in the enterprises of village improvement societies, — yes, even in the genealogical societies, and in the provincial clubs. I mean also the present form of that spirit which has originated, endowed, and fostered the colleges and universities of our Western towns, cities, and states, and which is so well shown throughout our country in our American pride in local institutions of learning. Of course, we have always had something of this provincialism. It is assuming new forms amongst us. I want to emphasize how much good it can do in training us to higher forms of loyalty.

That such provincialism is a good national trait to possess, the examples of Germany and of Great Britain, in their decidedly contrasting but equally important ways, can show us. The English village, the English country life, the Scotsman's love for his own native

province, — these are central features in determining the sort of loyalty upon which the
British Empire as a whole has depended.
Germany, like ourselves, has suffered much
from sectionalism. But even to-day the German national consciousness presupposes and
depends upon a highly developed provincial
life and loyalty. One of the historical weaknesses of France has been such a centralization of power and of social influence about
Paris as has held in check the full development of the dignity of provincial consciousness
in that country. Now, in our country we do
not want any mutual hatred of sections. But
we do want a hearty growth of provincial
ideals. And we want this growth just for
the sake of the growth of a more general and
effective patriotism. We want to train national loyalty through provincial loyalty. We
want the ideals of the various provinces of
our country to be enriched and made definite,
and then to be strongly represented in the
government of the nation. For, I insist, it is
not the sect, it is not the labor-union, it is not

the political partisan organization, but it is the widely developed provincial loyalty which is the best mediator between the narrower interests of the individual and the larger patriotism of our nation. Further centralization of power in the national government, without a constantly enriched and diversified provincial consciousness, can only increase the estrangement of our national spirit from its own life. On the other hand, history shows that if you want a great people to be strong, you must depend upon provincial loyalties to mediate between the people and their nation.

The present tendency to the centralization of power in our national government seems to me, then, a distinct danger. It is a substitution of power for loyalty. *To the increase of a wise provincialism in our country, I myself look for the best general social means of training our people in loyalty to loyalty.* But of course such training in loyalty to loyalty must largely be a matter of the training of individuals, and to the problem of individual training for loyalty our next lecture will be devoted.

VI
TRAINING FOR LOYALTY

LECTURE VI

TRAINING FOR LOYALTY

TWO objections which have been expressed to me by hearers of the foregoing lectures of this course deserve a word of mention here, as I begin the present discussion of the work of training individuals for a loyal life.

I

The first of these objections concerns my use of the term "loyalty." "Why," so the objection runs, "why can you not avoid the endless repetition of your one chosen term, 'loyalty'? Why would not other words, such as fidelity, devotion, absorption, trustworthiness, faithfulness, express just as well the moral quality to which you give the one name that you have employed?"

The second objection concerns my definition of the term "loyalty," and is closely connected with the first objection. It runs as follows: "Why do you insist that the cause which the loyal man serves must be a *social* cause? Why might one not show the same essential moral quality that you define, when the cause that he serves is something quite unearthly, or something earthly but quite unsocial? Saint Simeon on his pillar, Buddha seeking enlightenment under his lonely tree, the Greek geometer attempting to square the circle, — were they not as faithful as your loyal man is? And were their causes social causes?"

I reply to these objections together. I have defined my present usage of the popular term "loyalty" in my own distinctly technical way. Loyalty so far means for us, in these lectures, the willing, the thoroughgoing, and the practical devotion of a self to a cause. And a cause means, in these lectures, something that is conceived by its loyal servant as unifying the lives of various human begins into one life. Now, I know of no other word whose popular usage comes closer than does that of the good old word "loyalty" to embodying the meaning that I have given to the term. I think, then, that I have a right to my technical definition. It is based upon popular usage, and goes beyond that usage only in a very natural way. I intend soon to show you that we are now ready to substitute for this first technical definition another and a still more significant definition which will reveal to us, for the first time, the true spirit of the enterprise in which all the loyal are actually engaged. But I can reach this higher definition only through the simpler definition. To that, inadequate as it is, my discussion must cling until we are ready for something better.

Granting, however, my own definition of my term, I cannot easily use any other popular or philosophical term in the same way. I cannot substitute the word "devotion" for the term "loyalty, " since loyalty is to my mind a very special kind of devotion. A man might be devoted to the pursuit of pleasure; but that would not make him loyal. Fidelity, again, is, in my own account, but one aspect of loyalty. Loyalty includes fidelity, but means more, since, besides fidelity, decisiveness and the acceptance of a cause also belong to loyalty; and the fidelity of a dog to his master is only a pathetic hint of loyalty, or a fragment of the disposition that, in human beings, expresses itself in the full reasonableness of loyal life. The same comment holds in case of the word "faithfulness." As for *absorption*, the loyal are absorbed in their cause, but the angry man is absorbed in his passion. Yet such absorption is not what I have in mind. The loyal, again, possess *trustworthiness*, but a watch may also be trustworthy; and that word ill expresses the voluntary nature of the spirit of loyalty.

I cannot find, then, another term to meet my purpose. My usage of this term is justified mainly by that simplification of our conceptions of the moral life which our theory has made possible.

As for my insistence upon the social aspect of the loyal life, that insistence implies two assertions about such cases as those of the lonely saint on the pillar, or Buddha seeking enlightenment, or the geometer trying to solve his problem. The first assertion is that all such lonely enterprises have moral value only when they are indeed a part of one's service of the cause of humanity. The saint on the pillar was presumably trying to add to the store of merits which the universal church was supposed to possess. If so, he had a social cause which he served; namely, the church,—the mystic union of all the faithful. His cause may have been wrongly conceived by him, but it was, in our sense, a cause, and a social one. The Buddha of the legend was seeking to save not only himself but mankind. He was loyal, therefore, in our sense. As for the geometer, his search for the solution of his problem concerned one of the deepest common interests of the human mind; namely, an interest in the discovery and possession of rational truth. Truth is for everybody; and it unifies the lives of all men. Whoever seeks for a truth, as important as geometrical truth is, and seeks it with a serious devotion, has a social cause. And no utterly lonely devotion to anything is morally worthy of a human being.

My second assertion as to the social aspect of causes is this. Sometimes men have indeed sought to serve God in an actually unsocial way, and have been devoted to a world of unseen and superhuman beings. But such beings, if they are real and are worthy of a moral devotion at all, are worthy of the devotion of all mankind; and in such devotion, if it is indeed justified, all men may be blessed. The worship of the gods, even when a lonely worshipper has expressly tried not to think of his fellows, has therefore always implied a loyalty to the cause of one's own people, or else of mankind at large. The Christian's devotion to God is inseparably bound up with his loyalty to the mystic union of the faithful in the church. The non-social aspect of genuine worship is therefore but apparent. Religion seeks a certain fulfilment of the purposes of the moral life, — a fulfilment which we are hereafter to study. On the other hand, loyalty itself, as a devotion to a cause which unifies many human lives, is, as we shall see, profoundly religious in its spirit. For men, viewed merely as natural phenomena, are many, and mutually conflicting creatures. Loyalty aims at their unity, and such unity, as we shall see, is always something that has its supernatural meaning. In brief, then, to worship divine powers in a genuinely ethical spirit, is always to serve a cause which is also, in the human sense, social,—the cause of the state, or of the church, or of humanity; while, on the other hand, loyally to serve causes is to aim to give human life a supernatural,—an essentially divine meaning.

And these are the reasons why I have insisted upon the social aspect of loyalty.

Bear, then, I pray you, with my too often repeated term; accept its apparently too narrow definition. We are on the way towards a view of the spiritual unity of all human life, — a view which may serve to justify this technical usage of a term, this long dwelling upon the details of the moral life, these seemingly commonplace comments upon social problems.

II

How shall individuals be trained for a loyal life? That is the question of the present lecture. In trying to answer this question I shall first dwell, briefly, and very inadequately, upon the place that a training for loyalty should occupy in the education of the young. Then I shall speak of the way in which mature people are trained for such forms of loyalty as belong to the actual business of the social world.

Whether you like my use of terms or not, you will agree that training the young for a willing and thoroughgoing devotion of the self to a social cause, must be a long and manifold task. Before true loyalty can appear in any but rather crude and fragmentary forms in the life of a growing human being, a long discipline of the whole mind must have preceded. One must have become capable of conceiving what a social cause is. One must have learned decisiveness and fidelity through an elaborate general preparation of the will. Therefore, while the beginnings of loyalty extend far back into the life of childhood, its full development must belong to mature years. Affection, obedience, a gradually increasing persistence in wholesome activities, a growing patience and self-control, all these, in the natural growth of a human being, are preliminaries to the more elaborate forms of loyalty. By themselves they are not loyalty. In accordance with the general trend of modern educational theory, we therefore naturally point out that, in training children for future loyalty, teachers must avoid trying to awaken any particular sort of loyalty before its fitting basis is laid, and before a sufficient age has been reached. The basis in question involves a rich development of social habits. The age for true and systematic loyalty can hardly precede adolescence. One must obtain the material for a moral personality before a true conscience can be won. Conscience, as we have seen, is the flower and not the root of the moral life.

But there is one contribution which childhood early makes to a possible future loyalty, — a contribution which we sometimes fail to take sufficiently into account. That contribution is the well-known disposition to idealize heroes and adventures, to live an imaginary life, to have ideal comrades, and to dream of possible great enterprises. I have for years insisted, along with many others who have studied our educational problems, that these arts of idealization which childhood so often and so spontaneously practises, are not only in themselves fascinating and joyous, but are also a very important preliminary to that power to conceive the true nature of social causes upon which later loyalty depends. If I have never been fascinated in childhood by my heroes and by the wonders of life, it is harder to fascinate me later with the call of duty. Loyalty, as we have already seen, and as we have yet further to see, is an idealizing of human life, a communion with invisible aspects of our social existence. Too great literalness in the interpretation of human relations is, therefore, a foe to the development of loyalty. If my neighbor is to me merely a creature of a day, who walks and eats and talks and buys and sells, I shall never learn to be loyal to his cause and to mine. But the child who plays with ideal comrades, or who idealizes with an unconscious wisdom our literal doings and his own, is, in his own way, getting glimpses of that real spiritual world whose truth and whose unity we have hereafter more fully to consider. It is in his fantasies, then, that a child begins to enter into the kingdom of heaven. Such fantasies may need to be carefully guarded. They may take a dangerous or even a disastrous turn in the life of one or another child. But in their better phases they are not mere illusions and are great blessings. They are prophecies of the coming of conscience, and of a possible union with the world of an actually divine truth.

Yet since loyalty involves conduct, such

fantasies of childhood are indeed but a preparation for loyalty. And higher loyalty belongs later. But in normal childhood there do indeed appear, in a fragmentary way, forms of conduct which already include a simple, but, so far as it goes, an actual loyalty to the causes the child already understands. You all know some of these forms. The members of a gang of boys, sometimes of bad boys, show a certain loyalty to the cause represented by the gang. School children develop the code of honor that forbids the telling of tales to the teacher. Truthfulness becomes a conscious virtue early in normal childhood, and has its own childish casuistry, — often an amusing one.

The rule, of course, regarding all such childhood beginnings of loyalty is that we 'should always respect whatever is in the least socially tolerable about the expressions of even the crudest loyalty. The parent or teacher who trifles with the code of honor of children by encouraging the talebearer, or by even requiring that a child should become an informer, is simply encouraging disloyalty. He outrages the embryonic conscience of his young charges.

For the rest, children appreciate the loyalty or disloyalty of our conduct towards them sooner than they can define their own duty. And the one who would train for loyalty must therefore be, in his dealings with children, peculiarly scrupulous about his own loyalty.

III

But after all, whatever be the best training of childhood for a coming moral life, the rapid development of loyalty itself belongs to adolescence, just as the outcome of that development is reached only in mature life. Upon the importance of youth as the natural period for training in more elaborate forms of loyal conduct, our recent authority regarding adolescence, President Stanley Hall, has insisted. In normal youth various forms of loyalty, of a highly complex character, appear with a great deal of spontaneity. Two of these forms have become important in the life

of the youth of many nations, and certainly in the life of our own American youth to-day. The one form is loyalty to the fraternal organization,—very generally to a secret fraternity. The other form is loyalty to one's own side in an athletic contest, or to one's college or other institution, viewed as an athletic entity.

Both of these forms of loyalty have their excesses, and lead to well-known abuses. The secret fraternities may become organizations for general mischief and disorder; the athletic contests may involve overmuch passion, and may even do harm to the general loyalty by fostering the spirit of unfair play. Now, it is notable that both of these sorts of abuses increase when the fraternities and the athletic organizations are imitated in the lower schools by the children. The resulting dangers show that loyalty ought not to be a prematurely forced plant. It should grow, in its various forms, in its due time. Hence those in charge of our secondary schools should not be misled by their knowledge of the preciousness of loyalty into encouraging an overhasty development of secret fraternities and of fully formed athletic organizations amongst those who are not old enough to reap the fruits of such forms of loyalty. The coming of true loyalty may be seriously hindered by the too early organization of the perfectly natural gang of boys into some too elaborate social structure. Harm has been done of late years by too much aping of athletic and fraternity life in connection with the lower grades of schools.

But when youth is fairly reached, and the secret fraternity and the athletic organization become spontaneously prominent, it is plain that our efforts to train our youth to a higher life must recognize these natural types of loyalty, but must do so without overemphasizing their cruder features. We must always build upon what we have; and therefore any unnecessary hostility to the fraternities and to the athletic life is profoundly objectionable. But the most unhappy features of the athletic, and in some measure of the fraternity, life in our colleges and universities are due to the false social prominence which the public opinion of those who have nothing to do with college life often forces upon our youth. The athletic evils, such as they are, of our academic world, are not due to the college students themselves nearly so much as to the absurd social prominence which the newspapers and the vast modern crowds give to contests which ought to be cheerful youthful sports, wherein a natural loyalty is to be trained, but wherein a national prominence of the games and the contestants is utterly out of place. It is as absurd to overemphasize such matters as it is wicked to interfere unnecessarily with any other aspect of youthful moral development. It is the extravagant publicity of our intercollegiate sports which is responsible for their principal evils. Leave wholesome youth to their natural life, not irritated and not aroused to unwise emotions by the exaggerated comments of the press, and our athletic organizations would serve their proper function of training the muscles as well as the souls of our youth to loyalty. As for the fraternities, — the false social prominence which their graduate members sometimes force upon them is a distinct hindrance to the work that they can do in training youth for a loyal life.

Fair play in sport is a peculiarly good instance of loyalty. And in insisting upon the spirit of fair play, the elders who lead and who organize our youthful sports can do a great work for the nation. The coach, or the other leader in college sports, to whom fair play is not a first concern, is simply a traitor to our youth and to our nation. If the doctrine of these lectures is right, we can see with what stupendous human interests he is trifling.

As to other ways in which the loyalty of our youth can be trained, we still too much lack, in this country, dignified modes of celebrating great occasions. Once the Fourth of July was a day for training patriotic loyalty; it has now degenerated, and is probably irretrievably lost to the cause of true loyalty. Memorial Day and our national Thanksgiving Day are our best holidays for expressing loyalty to the community and to the nation. Let us cherish ·

them, and preserve them from desecration. But with us both holidays and public ceremonials have a certain democratic tendency to degeneration. We need more means for symbolizing loyalty, both in public monuments and in ceremonials, as well as in forms of common public service to our community. European nations glorify the army as a practical teacher of loyalty to the youth. The loyalty thus won is mingled with the war-spirit, and is therefore dear bought. But we unquestionably need substitutes for military service as a means of training for a loyal life. It belongs to the task of our social leaders to invent and to popularize such substitutes. Herein lies one of the great undertakings of the future.

IV

The true sphere of a complete loyalty is mature life. We constantly need, all of us, individual training in the art of loyalty. How is this work accomplished in the social order? In answering this question, let history and our daily social experience be our guides.

The main lessons that these guides teach us, as I think, are three: First, our loyalty is trained and kept alive by the influence of personal leaders. Secondly, the higher forms of training for loyalty involve a momentous process which I shall call the Idealizing of the Cause. Thirdly, loyalty is especially perfected through great strains, labors, and sacrifices in the service of the cause.

Of the three factors here mentioned, the first and second are inseparable and universal. If we are to be made loyal, we want personal leaders, and highly idealized causes. In exceptional cases a man may seem to be his own sole leader in loyalty. But this is rare. Always, to be sure, a loyal man uses his own leadership, since, as we saw in our fourth lecture, his conscience is his leader. But usually he needs the aid of other personal leaders besides himself. As for the idealizing of the cause, —I have called it a momentous process. How momentous we shall soon see. For it is by this process that we are introduced into the true spiritual world.

Let me illustrate my theses. We are all familiar with the history of clubs and of sectarian social organizations generally. Now how are these social enterprises, good or evil, made to succeed?

You all know that if a club or a sect is to be begun, or if a political or social movement is to be rendered effective, two things are necessary: first, a leader, or a group of leaders, eager, enthusiastic, convinced, or, at the worst, capable of speaking as if they were convinced, — leaders persistent, obstinate, and in their own fitting way aggressive; and, secondly, a cause that can be idealized so that, when the leaders talk of it in their glowing exhortations, it seems to be a sort of supernatural being, in one sense impersonal, but in another sense capable of being personified, an exalted but still personally interesting spiritual power. The two aspects of loyalty, the personal and the seemingly superpersonal, must thus be emphasized together.

Consider, in particular, the process of making almost any new club succeed. Some group

270

of persons, sometimes a single leader, must be found, willing to devote time and energy to directing the new organization. The leader or leaders must believe the enterprise worth while, must proclaim its importance in vigorous terms, and must patiently stand by the club through all the doubtful first period of its existence. But the personal influence of these leaders cannot be enough to arouse any genuine loyalty in the members of the club, unless the organization itself can be made to appear as a sort of ideal personality, of a higher than merely human type. If the leaders impress their companions as being people who are concerned merely with their own private importance, they in vain persist in their propaganda. In that case the club is nicknamed as their particular pet or as their fad; one makes light of their energy, one maligns their motives, and the club crumbles into nothing. In order to succeed, the leaders must give to the club the character of a sort of ideal entity, often of an improvised mythological goddess, who is to be conceived as favoring her devotees,

as bestowing upon them extraordinary social
or spiritual benefits. Even the convivial festivals of the club, if such festivals there be,
must have some sort of ceremonial dignity
about them,—a dignity such as suggests the
impersonal or superpersonal rank of the club
as an ideal. The club must become a cause,
in whose service the members are one. If it is
a reform club, or other body engaged in a
propaganda, then social interests that lie outside of the boundaries of the club's separate
being serve to define this cause; the club is
then merely an instrument to further a loyalty
that is intelligible apart from the existence of
this very instrument; and in such a case the
leaders of the club have mainly to insist effec-
tively upon the importance of this already existing loyalty. But if the club is to be an end in
itself, — an organization that exists for its own
sake and for the sake of its own members,—
the process of learning to ascribe to the new
club the ideal dignity of a common cause is
sometimes a difficult process. The devices
used by the leaders are, upon occasion, very

direct. One simply calls the club an ideal; one personifies it in various poetical ways; and one praises it as a sort of superhuman being. Or, more practically still, one incorporates the club, endows it with a legal personality, and makes it a property owner. But other devices are more indirect. Club ceremonials and festivals, some more or less rudimentary club ritual, perhaps also the various familiar devices of the secret societies, the air of mystery, club emblems and symbols, —all serve to give to the club the appearances, at least, of a fitting cause for the exercise of loyalty. Another indirect device consists in naming the club after famous or beloved people, now dead, whose honor and whose memory idealize the new organization. Or, again, one arbitrarily calls the club ancient and dignifies it by a more or less conscious myth about its past. All such devices serve to call out loyalty in ways that may be comparatively trivial, but that may also be of a very profound significance, if the new organization is actually a fitting object of loyalty.

With proper changes the foregoing account applies to the plans that are useful in establishing a new religious sect. Always you find the same union of personal enthusiasm on the part of leaders with a disposition to define the ideal of the new organization in terms that transcend the limits of individual human life. Man, even when he is a member of a purely convivial social body, is prone to try to conceive both his own life, and also that of this social body, in superhuman terms. Experience thus shows that a procedure of the sort just described does succeed, in many cases, in training people — sometimes small groups, sometimes great bodies of men — to new forms of loyalty.

The plans whereby an actually ancient institution is kept in possession of the loyalty of its own natural servants do not in their essence differ from the ones just characterized. The loyalty of a body of alumni to their university is a classic instance of a loyalty kept alive by the union of an institution with the personality of its living leaders. Even so, the loyalty of the sons of a subjugated nationality, such as the Irish or the Poles, to their country, is kept alive through precisely such an union of the influence of individual leaders with the more impersonal reverence for the idealized, although no longer politically existent nationality.

You see, so far, how the personal leaders and the superhuman cause are inseparable in the training of loyalty. The cause comes to be idealized partly because the leaders so vigorously insist that it is indeed ideal. On the other hand, the leaders become and remain personally efficacious by reason of the dignity that the cause confers upon them. Were they considered apart from their cause, they would seem to be merely ambitious propagandists, seeking gain or notoriety. To those without the range of their personal influence, they often seem such. Yet if they did not speak for the cause, and so give to it the life of their personal enthusiasm, nobody would be taught to regard their cause as ideal. The cause thus needs to become incarnate, as it were, in the persons of the leaders; but the leaders get their personal influence through the fact that they seem to be incarnations of the cause.

Facts of this sort are familiar. You can observe them whenever you attend an anniversary meeting, or other such ceremonial, of your own club, and whenever you listen to those who represent any successful propaganda. But how vastly significant such facts may be in determining the lives of whole generations and nations and races of men, you can only judge if you read the general history of humanity in the light of the principles now pointed out. If our philosophy of loyalty has any truth, the history of human loyalty concerns whatever is most important in the annals of mankind. And the whole history of loyalty is the history of the inseparable union of the personal influence of leaders with the tendency to idealize causes.

V

But the idealization of the cause, although never possible without the aid of living persons, may also depend upon still other factors than the direct personal influence of leaders. When we consider the general history of loyalty amongst men, our attention is soon attracted to a deeply instructive process whereby, in certain cases, — some of them very great and wonderful cases, — causes have been idealized not only by the personal influence of the leaders, but also by certain deeply pathetic motives to which the leaders could constantly appeal. I refer to the process illustrated by the history of lost causes.

I referred a moment ago to the loyalty of the Irish and of the Poles to their own lost nationalities. Now such loyalty to a lost cause may long survive, not merely in the more or less unreal form of memories and sentiments, but in a genuinely practical way. And such loyalty to a lost cause may be something that far transcends the power of any mere habit. New plans, endless conspiracies, fruitful social enterprises, great political organizations, — yes, in the extreme case, — new religions, may grow up upon the basis of such a loyalty to a cause whose worldly fortunes seem lost, but whose vitality may outlast centuries, and may involve much novel growth of opinion, of custom, and of ideals.

The most notable religious development which the world has ever seen, the religion of Israel, together with its successor, Christianity, —this whole religious evolution, —is, as we must here point out, the historical result of a national loyalty to a lost cause. The political unity of all the tribes of Israel, attained but for a moment, so to speak, under David and Solomon, and then lost from the visible world of history, survived as an ideal. Only as such a lost ideal could this conception of what Israel once was and ought again to be inspire the Old Testament prophets to speak the word of the Lord regarding the way of righteousness whereby, as the prophets held, the prosperity of Israel was to be restored. Only this same lost political ideal, and this resulting discovery of the prophetic theory of the divine government of human affairs, could lead over to that later religious interpretation and to that rewriting of the whole ancient history of Israel, which we now read in our Old Testament. Only upon the same basis could the Messianic idea come to be defined; and only thus could the prophetic doctrine of the universal future triumph of righteousness come to be formulated. And so through an historical process, every step of which depended upon a pathetic and yet glorious loyalty to a lost national cause, the ideals in question were at once universalized and intensified until, through Israel, all the nations of Christendom have been blessed. In consequence, to-day, in speaking of its own hopes of the salvation of mankind, and in describing its coming kingdom of heaven, Christianity still uses the familiar terms: Zion, the throne of David, Jerusalem,—terms whose original application was to places and to persons first made notable in their own time merely by reason of the petty tribal feuds of an obscure province. Thus loyalty, steadfast and yet developing through centuries, gradually transformed what were once seemingly insignificant matters of local politics into the most sacred concerns of a world religion.

Loyalty to lost causes is, then, not only a possible thing, but one of the most potent influences of human history. In such cases, the cause comes to be idealized through its very failure to win temporary and visible success. The result for loyalty may be vast. I need not remind you that the early Christian church itself was at first founded directly upon a loyalty to its own lost cause, —a cause which it viewed as heavenly just because here on earth the enemies seemed to have triumphed, and because the Master had departed from human vision. The whole history of Christianity is therefore one long lesson as to how a cause may be idealized through apparent defeat, and how even thereby loyalty may be taught to generation after generation of men, and may develop into endlessly new forms, and so may appeal to peoples to whom the cause in question was originally wholly strange. This history shows us how such a teaching and such an evolution of an idea may be furthered by what seems at first most likely to discourage loyalty, that is, by loss, by sorrow, by worldly defeat.

Loyalty to a lost cause, whatever the grade of dignity of the cause, depends in part, of course, upon the same motives which the simpler and more direct forms of loyalty employ.

But when a cause is lost in the visible world, and when, nevertheless, it survives in the hearts of its faithful followers, one sees more clearly than ever that its appeal is no longer to be fully met by any possible present deed. Whatever one can just now do for the cause is thus indeed seen to be inadequate. All the more, in consequence, does this cause demand that its followers should plan and work for the far-off future, for whole ages and æons of time; should prepare the way for their Lord, the cause, and make his paths straight. Activity becomes thus all the more strenuous, just because its consequences are viewed as so far-reaching and stupendous. Man's extremity is loyalty's opportunity. The present may seem dark. All the greater the work yet to be done. The distant future must be conquered. How vast the undertaking, —how vast, but therefore how inspiring!

All this larger and broader devotion of those loyal to a lost cause is colored and illuminated by strong emotion. Sorrow over what has been lost pierces deep into the hearts of the faithful. So much the more are these hearts stirred to pour out their devotion. Meanwhile, the glamour of memory is over the past. Whatever was commonplace about the former visible fortunes of the lost cause is now forgotten. For the memory of those who sorrow over loss is, as we all know, fond of precious myths, and views these myths as a form in which truth appears. In the great days that have passed away — in the days before the cause suffered defeat — there was indeed tragedy; but there was glory. Legend, often truer, — yes, as Aristotle said of poetry, more philosophical than history,—thus reads into that past not what the lost cause literally was, but what it meant to be. Its body is dead. But it has risen again. The imagination, chastened by all this grief, stirred by all this deep need, not only reforms the story of the past, but builds wonderful visions of what is yet to be.

Loyalty for the lost cause is thus attended by two comrades, grief and imagination. Yet loyalty, always strenuous and active, is not enervated by these deep emotions, nor yet confused by the wealth of these visions; but rather devotes itself to resolving upon what shall be. Grief it therefore transforms into a stimulating sense of need. If we have lost, then let us find. Loyalty also directs its deeds by the visions that imagination furnishes; and meanwhile it demands in turn that the imagination shall supply it with visions that can be translated into deeds. When it hears from the imagination the story of the coming triumph, it does not become passive. Rather does it say: Watch, for ye know not the day or the hour when the triumph of the cause is to come.

Hora novissima
Tempora pessima
Sunt, vigilemus.

This wonderful awakening from the prostration of grief to the stern but fascinating resolve to live and to be active for the lost cause, this freeing of the imagination through the very agony of missing the dear presence in the visible world, and this complete control both of such passion and of such imagination through the will to make all things work together for the good of the cause, — all this is the peculiar privilege of those who are loyal to a cause which the world regards as lost, and which the faithful view as ascended into a higher realm, certain to come again in renewed might and beauty. Thus may grief minister to loyalty.

And I may add, as an obvious truth of human nature, that loyalty is never raised to its highest levels without such grief. For what one learns from experience of grief over loss is precisely the true link between loyalty as a moral attitude, and whatever is eternally valuable in religion. One begins, when one serves the lost causes, to discover that, in some sense, one ought to devote one's highest loyalty precisely to the causes that are too good to be visibly realized at any one moment of this poor wretched fleeting time world in which we see and touch and find mere things, mere sensations, mere feelings of the moment. Loyalty wants the cause in its unity; it seeks, therefore, something essentially superhuman. And therefore, as you see, loyalty is linked with religion. In its highest reaches it always is, therefore, the service of a cause that is just now lost — and lost because the mere now is too poor a vehicle for the presentation of that ideal unity of life of which every form of loyalty is in quest. Loyalty to loyalty, that cause of causes upon which I have so much insisted in the foregoing, is indeed just now in far too many ways a lost cause amongst men. But that is the fault of the men, not of the cause. Let us rejoice that we can serve a cause of which the world, as it is, is not yet worthy.

The history of the lost causes is instructive, however, not only as showing us a new aspect of the value of loyalty, namely, what I have just called the link between loyalty and religion, but also as showing us something of the way in which grief, and imagination, and the stirring of our whole human nature to its very depths, through loss and through defeat, have served in the past as means of training in loyalty. This school of adversity has often been a hard one. But the loyalty that has been trained in this school has produced for us some of humanity's most precious spiritual treasures. Thus, then, through personal leaders and through suffering, loyalty learns to idealize its cause.

VI

What is the lesson of all the foregoing when we ask: How shall we ourselves seek training in loyalty?

The first answer is obvious: Whatever our cause, we need personal leaders. And how shall we be surest of finding such personal leaders? Shall we look exclusively to those who are fellow-servants of our own chosen special causes? We all do this. Yet this is often not enough. Familiarity and personal misunderstandings often interfere with the guidance that our fellow-servants give us. We need the wider outlook. Close friendships are amongst the most powerful supports of loyalty. Yet when people confine themselves to regarding their close friends as their leaders in loyalty, they often become narrow and forget the cause of universal loyalty. Much of the art of loyalty, consequently, depends upon training yourself to observe the loyal who are all about you, however remote their cause is from yours, however humble their lives. It is well also, whenever you have to fight, to learn the art of honoring your opponent's loyalty, even if you learn of it mainly through feeling the weight and the sharpness of his sword. "It is a deep cut; but a loyal enemy was he who could give it to me" —to think in such terms is to lighten the gloom of conflict with what may sometimes be more precious than a transient victory; for at such moments of honoring the loyally dangerous enemy, we begin to learn that all the loyal are in spirit serving, however unwittingly, the same universal cause. To be sure, when men have once sufficiently learned that lesson, they cease to fight. But while fighting lasts, if you cannot love your enemy, it is a beautiful thing to be able to enjoy the sight of his loyalty.

But men have not to fight one another in order to display loyalty. Open your eyes, then, to observe better the loyalty of the peaceful, as well as of the warriors. Consider especially the loyalty of the obscure, of the humble, of your near neighbors, of the strangers who by chance come under your notice. For such exemplars of loyalty you always have. Make them your leaders. Regard every loyal man as your leader in the service of the cause of universal loyalty.

VII

But our review of the history of loyalty taught us another lesson. We need not only leaders. We need to idealize our causes; that is, to see in them whatever most serves to link them to the cause of universal loyalty.

And the procedure whereby our causes are to be idealized is one involving a range of possible experiences and activities far too vast to be adequately surveyed in our present discussion. Here belong all those practically valuable relations between loyalty and art, and between loyalty and religion, which the history of mankind illustrates and which we can use in our own training for loyalty.   Art supports loyalty whenever it associates our cause with beautiful objects, whenever it sets before us the symbols of our cause in any worthy expression, and whenever, again, by showing us any form of the beautiful, it portrays to us that very sort of learning and unity that loyalty ceaselessly endeavors to bring into human life. Thus viewed, art may be a teacher of loyalty. To say this is in no wise to prejudge the famous question regarding the main purpose of art, and the relation of this purpose of art to the moral life.   I am attempting here no theory of art.   But it belongs to our present province merely to insist that part of our education in loyalty is to be won through whatever love of beauty and whatever knowledge of the beautiful we possess. The monuments of any cause that possesses monuments should associate our love of this cause with our love for beauty. Our personal causes, if they are worthy at all, need beautiful symbols to express to us their preciousness. Whatever is beautiful appears to us to embody harmonious relations. And the practical search for harmony of life constitutes loyalty. And thus training for loyalty includes the knowledge of the beautiful.

Still more universal in its efficacy as an idealizer of private and personal causes is religion. In how far a genuinely religious experience results from loyalty, and in how far loyalty bears witness to any religiously significant truth, we have hereafter to see. Our closing lectures will deal with the bearing of loyalty upon religion. But we have here to mention, in passing, the converse relation; namely, the influence of religion upon loyalty. We have to point out how large a part of the function of religion in human affairs consists in the idealizing of our loyalties, by linking our causes, whatever they are, to a world which seems to us to be superhuman.

VIII

Art and religion, however, are not our only means for teaching ourselves to view our personal causes as linked with universal human interests, and with an unseen superhuman world. Sorrow, defeat, disappointment, failure, whenever these result from our efforts to serve a cause, may all be used to teach us the same lesson. How such lessons have been taught to humanity at large, the history of those lost causes which have been, even because of the loss, transformed into causes of permanent and world-wide importance, has now shown us. This lesson of the history of the lost causes is, however, one that has deep importance for our individual training. We do not always read this lesson aright. To keep our loyalty steadfast through defeat is something that we often view as a sort of extra strain upon loyalty, —the overcoming of a painful hindrance to loyalty. We ought not so to view the matter. Defeat and sorrow, when they are incurred in the service of a cause, ought rather to be a positive aid to loyalty. If we rightly view them, they will prove to be such an aid. For they enable us to see whether we have really given ourselves to the cause, or whether what we took for loyalty was a mere flare of sanguine emotion. When sorrow over a defeat in the service of our cause reverberates all through us, it can be made to reveal whatever loyalty we have. Let us turn our attention to this revelation, even while we suffer. We shall then know for what we have been living. And whoever, once deliberately dwelling upon his cause at a moment of defeat, does not find the cause dearer to him because of his grief, has indeed yet to learn what loyalty is. The cause, furthermore, when viewed in the light of our sorrow over our loss of its present fortunes, at once tends to become idealized,— as the lost throne of David was idealized by Israel, and as the departed Master's cause was idealized by the early church.

The disciples, in the well-known story, say concerning their lost Master to the stranger whom they meet on the lonely road to Emmaus: "We had trusted that it was he who should have redeemed Israel." But soon after "their eyes were opened, and they knew him, and he vanished out of their sight." Amongst all the legends of the risen Lord, this one most completely expresses the spirit of that loyalty which, triumphing even through defeat, winning the spirit even through the loss of a visible presence, was thereafter to conquer its world.

Now, the lesson of such experiences, as history records them, relates not merely to great movements and to mankind at large. It is a personal lesson. It concerns each one of us. I repeat: View your sorrow by itself, and it is a blind and hopeless fact; view your cause in the light of your sorrow, and the cause becomes transfigured. For you learn hereby that it was not this or that fortune, nor even this or that human life which constituted your cause. There was from the beginning, about your cause, something that to human vision seems superpersonal, unearthly as well as earthly. Now the memory of whatever is lost about your cause is peculiarly adapted to bring to your consciousness what this superpersonal element has been. I have already mentioned the merely psychological aspects of the process that, in such cases, goes on. The glamour which memory throws about the past, the awakening of the imagination when some visible presence is removed, the stimulating reaction from the first stroke of sorrow whenever we are able once more to think of our cause itself, the transformation of our own ideas about the cause, by virtue of the very fact that, since our loss has so changed life, the cause can no longer be served in the old way, and must be the object of new efforts, and so of some new form of devotion,— all these are the idealizing motives which are present when defeat comes. I insist, — human loyalty can never be perfected without such sorrow. Regard defeat and bereavement, therefore, as loyalty's opportunity. Use them deliberately as means for idealizing the cause, and so far bringing your personal cause into closer touch with the cause of universal loyalty.

The most familiar of all those blows of fortune which seem to us, for the moment, to make our personal cause a lost cause, is death, when it comes to those with whom our personal cause has so far been bound up. And yet what motive in human life has done more to idealize the causes of individuals than death has done? Death, viewed as a mere fact of human experience, and as a merely psychological influence, has been one of the greatest idealizers of human life. The memory of the dead idealizes whatever interest the living have in former days shared with the departed. Reverence for the dead dignifies the effort to carry on the work that they began, or that, if they died in childhood, our fond desire would have had them live to do. From the beginning a great portion of the religious imagination of mankind has centred about the fact of death. And the same motive works to-day in the minds of all the loyal, whatever their faith.

Idealize your cause. This has been our

maxim for the present aspect of our personal training in loyalty. I have offered merely some hints as to how this maxim may be carried into effect. How science can join with art and with religion, how joyous friendly intercourse can in its own place coöperate with our experiences of sorrow to teach us the lessons of idealizing our common causes,—all this I can only indicate.

And thus we have before us two of the methods whereby individual loyalty is trained. The deliberate fixing of our attention upon the doings of loyal people, the deliberate use of those methods of human nature which tend to idealize our cause,—these are means for training in loyalty.

Yet one method remains,—it is the most commonplace, yet often the hardest of all. Loyalty means giving the Self to the Cause. And the art of giving is learned by giving. Strain, endurance, sacrifice, toil,—the dear pangs of labor at the moments when perhaps defeat and grief most seem ready to crush our powers, and when only the very vehemence of labor itself saves us from utter despair,— these are the things that most teach us what loyalty really is. I need not enlarge here upon an ancient and constantly repeated lesson of life, — a lesson which is known to all of you. The partisans of war often glorify war as a moralizer of humanity, because, as they say, only the greatest strains and dangers can teach men true loyalty. I do not think that war is needed for such lessons. The loyalty of the most peaceful enables us all to experience, sooner or later, what it means to give, whatever it was in our power to give, for the cause, and then to see our cause take its place, to human vision, amongst the lost causes. When such experiences come, let us face them without hesitation. For all these things together,— our personal friends who inspire us to the service of our own causes, the hosts of the loyal whom we know so little, but who constitute the invisible church of those who live in the spirit, the griefs that teach us the glory of what our human vision has lost from its field, the imagination that throws over all the range of human life its idealizing light, the labors that leave us breathless, the crushing defeats that test our devotion, — well, these, these are all only the means and the ministers whereby we are taught to enter the realm of spiritual truth.

VII

LOYALTY, TRUTH, AND REALITY

LECTURE VII

LOYALTY, TRUTH, AND REALITY

IN closing my last lecture I said that whatever trains us in the arts of loyalty enables us to enter into a world of spiritual truth. These words were intended to indicate that the loyal life has another aspect than the one hitherto most emphasized in these lectures. Our foregoing account has been deliberately one-sided. We have been discussing the moral life as if one could define a plan of conduct without implying more about man's place in the real universe than we have yet made explicit in these lectures. Hence our discussion, so far, is open to obvious objections.

For, in talking about the good of loyalty, we have indeed appealed to human experience to show us wherein that good consists. But our very appeal also showed us that loyalty is good for a man precisely because he believes that his cause itself, even apart from his ser-

301

vice, is good, and that both his cause and its goodness are realities, founded in facts which far transcend his individual life and his personal experience. Now, one may well doubt whether this belief of a loyal man is, in any individual case, a well-founded belief. And if it is not well founded, one may well question whether the loyal man's good is not, after all, an illusory good, which will vanish from his experience as soon as he becomes enlightened. Since any instance of loyalty is subject to this sceptical inquiry, one may doubt whether even what we have called the supreme cause, that of loyalty to loyalty, is a good cause. For any or all loyalties may be founded in illusion, and then it would be an illusion that the fostering of loyalty amongst men is a finally worthy undertaking.

I

Objections of this sort are best stated by those to whom they actually occur as serious difficulties regarding the discussions contained in the foregoing lectures. A dear friend of mine, without receiving any instigation from me to help me by such an act, has so aptly summed up the objections here in question, that I can best show you precisely where we now stand by reading to you a portion of a letter which he has written to me, after hearing the first portion of my account of the good of loyalty.

"'Loyalty to loyalty,'" writes my friend, "doesn't seem ultimate. Is it not loyalty to all *objects* of true loyalty that is our ultimate duty? The object, not the relation, — the universe and the devotion to it, not the devotion alone, is the object of our ultimate devotion. . . . Is it not the glory of this goal that lends dignity to all loyal search, — our own or that of others? It is because of this goal that we cheer on all to pursue it. . . . It is because of what we believe about the end of the various loyalties that we are so glad of all the loyalties which make it possible to attain that end. The port gives value to the courses steering for it. . . . Except for our knowledge of the value of their destination, and of

303

all life lived in quest of that destination, should we be anxious to urge all seekers along their courses? . . . Loyalty is a relation. . . . Can we be loyal to anything, ultimately, except the universe which is the object of all love and all knowledge?"

So far my friend's statement of his difficulty. As you will see, from these two closing lectures of my course which still remain, I cordially share my friend's objection to the definition of loyalty so far insisted upon in these lectures. Our definition of loyalty, and of its relation to the ultimate good which the loyal are seeking, has so far been inadequate. But, as I told you in the opening lecture, we deliberately began with an inadequate definition of the nature of loyalty. We were obliged to do so. I expressly said this in my opening statement. Why we were obliged to do so, and why, thus far in these lectures, we have confined ourselves to developing and to illustrating the consequences of this imperfect definition of loyalty, our closing lectures will of themselves, I hope, make clear.

A similar difficulty can be urged against any
mere moralism, that is, against any purely
ethical theory of the moral life. One wants
a doctrine of the real world, or a religion, to
help out one's ethics. For, as I have replied
to my friend, morality, viewed by itself, has
a character that can well be suggested by the
parable of the talents. The moral life, regarded simply as the moral life, is the service of a master who seems, to those who
serve him, to have gone away into a far
country. His servants have faith in him, but
the service of his cause always has, for the
moral, a certain mystery about it. They
can indeed become sure, apart from any solution of this mystery, that their own supreme
personal good lies in serving their lord. For
not otherwise can they find even the relative
peace that lies in a service of duty. But
those who serve are not thus altogether
secured against a pessimism regarding the
whole outcome of human endeavor. For if
loyalty is indeed our best, may not even this
best itself be a failure?

Or, to use further the similitude of the parable of the talents: It may be indeed our supreme good to serve the master who has gone into the far country. Yet we do not merely want to serve him; we want, like Job, to meet him face to face. Suppose that we should discover the master to be indeed unworthy or a phantom or a deceiver, would even this, our best good, the service of his cause, seem permanently valuable? Should we not say, some day: To serve him was our best chance of life; but after all even that service was vanity.

In any case, our loyalty implies a faith in the master, —an assurance that life, at its best, is indeed worth while. Our philosophy of loyalty must therefore include an attempt to see the master of life himself, and to find out whether in truth he is, what our loyalty implies that he is, a master worth serving.

To sum up: So far we have defined the moral life as loyalty, and have shown why the moral life is for us men the best life. But now we want to know what truth is behind and beneath the moral life. With my friendly correspondent, we want to see the relation of loyalty to the real universe.

II

What must be true about the universe if even loyalty itself is a genuine good, and not a merely inevitable human illusion?

Well, loyalty is a service of causes. A cause, if it really is what our definition requires, links various human lives into the unity of one life. Therefore, if loyalty has any basis in truth, human lives can be linked in some genuine spiritual unity. Is such unity a fact, or is our belief in our causes a mere point of view, a pathetic fallacy? Surely, if any man, however loyal, discovers that his cause is a dream, and that men remain as a fact sundered beings, not really linked by genuine spiritual ties, how can that man remain loyal? Perhaps his supreme good indeed lies in believing that such unities are real. But if this belief turns out to be an illusion, and if a man detects the illusion, can he any longer get the good out of loyalty?

And as for even this personal good that is to be got out of loyalty, we have all along seen that such good comes to a loyal man's mind in a very paradoxical way. A loyal man gets good, but since he gets it by believing that his cause has a real existence outside of his private self, and is of itself a good thing, he gets the fascination of loyalty not as a private delight of his own, but as a fulfilment of himself through self-surrender to an externally existing good, — through a willing abandonment of the seeking of his own delight. And so the loyal man's good is essentially an anticipation of a good that he regards as not his own, but as existent in the cause. The cause, however, is itself no one fellow-man, and no mere collection of fellow-men. It is a family, a country, a church, or is such a rational union of many human minds and wills as we have in mind when we speak of a science or an art. Now, can such causes contain any good which is not simply a collection of separate human experiences of pleasure or of satisfaction? Thus, then, both the reality and the good of a loyal man's cause must be objects of the loyal man's belief in order that he should be able to get the experience of loyalty. And if his loyalty is indeed well founded, there must be unities of spiritual life in the universe such that no one man ever, by himself, experiences these unities as facts of his own consciousness. And these higher unities of life must possess a degree and a type of goodness,—a genuine value, such that no one man, and no mere collection of men, can ever exhaustively experience this goodness, or become personally possessed of this value.

How paradoxical a world, then, must the real world be, if the faith of the loyal is indeed well founded! A spiritual unity of life, which transcends the individual experience of any man, must be real. For loyalty, as we have seen, is a service of causes that, from the human point of view, appear superpersonal. Loyalty holds these unities to be good. If loyalty is right, the real goodness of these causes is never completely manifested to any one man, or to any mere collection of men. Such goodness, then, if completely experienced at all, must be experienced upon some higher level of consciousness than any one human being ever reaches. If loyalty is right, social causes, social organizations, friendships, families, countries, yes, humanity, as you see, must have the sort of unity of consciousness which individual human persons fragmentarily get, but must have this unity upon a higher level than that of our ordinary human individuality.

Some such view, I say, must be held if we are to regard loyalty as in the end anything more than a convenient illusion. Loyalty has its metaphysical aspect. It is an effort to conceive human life in an essentially superhuman way, to view our social organizations as actual personal unities of consciousness, unities wherein there exists an actual experience of that good which, in our loyalty, we only partially apprehend. If the loyalty of the lovers is indeed well founded in fact, then they, as separate individuals, do not constitute the whole truth. Their spiritual union also has a personal, a conscious existence, upon a higher than human level. An analogous unity of consciousness, an unity superhuman in grade, but intimately bound up with, and inclusive of, our apparently separate personalities, must exist, if loyalty is well founded, wherever a real cause wins the true devotion of ourselves. Grant such an hypothesis, and then loyalty becomes no pathetic serving of a myth. The good which our causes possess, then, also becomes a concrete fact for an experience of a higher than human level. That union of self-sacrifice with self-assertion which loyalty expresses becomes a consciousness of our genuine relations to a higher social unity of consciousness in which we all have our being. For from this point of view we are, and we have our worth, by virtue of our relation to a consciousness of a type superior to the human type. And meanwhile the good of our loyalty is itself a perfectly concrete good, a good which is present to that higher experience, wherein our cause is viewed in its truth, as a genuine unity of life. And because of this fact we can straightforwardly say: We are loyal not for the sake of the good that we privately get out of loyalty, but for the sake of the good that the cause — this higher unity of experience — gets out of this loyalty. Yet our loyalty gives us what is, after all, our supreme good, for it defines our true position in the world of that social will wherein we live and move and have our being.

I doubt not that such a view of human life, — such an assertion that the social will is a concrete entity, just as real as we are, and of still a higher grade of reality than ourselves, — will seem to many of you mythical enough. Yet thus to view the unity of human life is, after all, a common tendency of the loyal. That fact I have illustrated in every lecture of this course. That such a view need not be mythical, that truth and reality can be conceived only in such terms as these, that our philosophy of loyalty is a rational part of a philosophy which must view the whole world as one unity of consciousness, wherein countless lesser unities are synthesized,—this is a general philosophical thesis which I must next briefly expound to you.

III

My exposition, as you see, must be, in any case, an attempt to show that the inevitable faith of the loyal — their faith in their causes, and in the real goodness of their causes — has truth, and since I must thus, in any case, discourse of truth, I propose briefly to show you that whoever talks of any sort of truth whatever, be that truth moral or scientific, the truth of common sense or the truth of a philosophy, inevitably implies, in all his assertions about truth, that the world of truth of which he speaks is a world possessing a rational and spiritual unity, is a conscious world of experience, whose type of consciousness is higher in its level than is the type of our human minds, but whose life is such that our life belongs as part to this living whole.

This world of truth is the one that you must define, so I insist, if you are to regard any proposition whatever as true, and are then to tell, in a reasonable way, what you mean by the truth of that proposition.

The world of truth is therefore essentially a world such as that in whose reality the loyal believe when they believe their cause to be real. Moreover, this truth world has a goodness about it, essentially like that which the loyal attribute to their causes. Truth seeking and loyalty are therefore essentially the same process of life merely viewed in two different aspects. Whoever is loyal serves what he takes to be a truth, namely, his cause. On the other hand, whoever seeks truth for its own sake fails of his business if he seeks it merely as a barren abstraction, that has no life in it. If a truth seeker knows his business, he is, then, in the sense of our definition, serving a cause which unifies our human life upon some higher level of spiritual being than the present human level. He is therefore essentially loyal. Truth seeking is a moral activity; and on the other hand, morality is wholly inadequate unless the light of eternal truth shines upon it.

This, I say, will be my thesis. Some of you will call it very mystical, or at least a very fantastic thesis. It is not so. It ought to be viewed as a matter of plain sense. It is, I admit, a thesis which many of the most distinguished amongst my colleagues, who are philosophers, nowadays view sometimes with amusement, and sometimes with a notable impatience. This way of regarding the world of truth, which I have just defined as mine, is especially and most vivaciously attacked by my good friends, the pragmatists, — a group of philosophers who have of late been disposed to take truth under their especial protection, as if she were in danger from the tendency of some people who take her too seriously.

When I mention pragmatism, I inevitably bring to your minds the name of one whom we all honor, — the philosopher who last year so persuasively stated, before the audience of this Institute, the pragmatist theory of philosophical method, and of the nature of truth. It is impossible for me to do any justice, within my limits, to the exposition which Professor James gave of his own theory of truth. Yet since the antithesis between his views and those which I have now to indicate to you may be in itself an aid to my own exposition, I beg you to allow me to use, for the moment, some of his assertions about the nature of truth as a means of showing, by contrast, how I find myself obliged to interpret the same problem. The contrast is accompanied, after all, by so much of deeper agreement that I can well hope that my sketch of the current situation in the philosophical controversies about truth may not seem to you merely a dreary report of differences of opinion.

Professor James, in discussing the nature of truth, in his recent book on pragmatism, begins, as some of you will remember, by accepting the classic definition of truth as the agreement of our ideas with reality. Whoever knows or possesses a truth has, then, in his mind, an idea, an opinion, a judgment, or some complex of such states of mind. If his views are true, then these his ideas or opinions are in agreement with something called reality. Thus, for instance, if a loyal man believes his cause, say, his friendship or his club or his nation, to be a reality, and if his belief is true, his loyal opinion is in agreement with the real world. So far, of course, all of you will accept the definition of truth here in question.

Professor James now goes on to point out that, in some cases, our ideas agree with what we call real things by copying those things. So, if, with shut eyes, you think of the clock on the wall, your image of the clock is a copy of its dial. But, as my colleague continues, our power to copy real objects by ideas of our own is obviously a very limited power. You believe that you have at least some true ideas about many objects which are far too complex or too mysterious for you to copy them. Your power to become sure that your ideas do copy the constitution of anything whatever which

exists outside of you is also very limited, because, after all, you never get outside of your
own experience to see what the real things
would be if taken wholly in themselves.
Hence, on the whole, one cannot say that the
agreement of our ideas with reality which
constitutes their truth is essentially such as to
demand that our ideas should be copies. For
we believe that we have true ideas even when
we do not believe them to be copies.

Moreover (and herewith we approach a
consideration which is, for my colleague's
theory of truth, very essential), not only
does truth not consist merely in copying facts;
but also truth cannot be defined in terms of
any other static or fixed relation between ideas
and facts. The only way to conceive that
agreement between ideas and facts which
constitutes truth is to think of the "practical
consequences" which follow from possessing
true ideas. "True ideas," in Professor
James's words, "lead us, namely, through the
acts and other ideas which they instigate, into
or up to or towards other parts of experience

with which we feel all the while that the original ideas remain in agreement. The connections and transitions come to us, from point to point, as being progressive, harmonious, satisfactory. This function of agreeable leading is what we mean by an idea's verification." So far my colleague's words. He goes on, in his account, to mention many illustrations of the way in which the truth of ideas is tested, both in the world of common sense, and in the world of science, by the usefulness, by the success, which attaches to the following out of true ideas to their actual empirical consequences. The wanderer lost in the woods gets true ideas about his whereabouts whenever he hits upon experiences and ideas which set him following the path which actually leads him home. In science, hypotheses are tested as to their truth, by considering what experiences they lead us to anticipate, and by then seeing whether these anticipations can be fulfilled in a satisfactory way. "True," says Professor James, "is the name for whatever idea starts the verification process." For instance, then, the verifiable scientific hypothesis, if once tested by the success of its results in experience, is in so far declared true. And similarly, the idea of following a given path in the woods in order to get home is declared true, if you follow the path and get home.

In consequence, every true idea is such in so far as it is useful in enabling you to anticipate the sort of experience that you want; and every idea that is useful as a guide of life is in so far true. The personal tests of usefulness, as of truth, are for every one of us personal and empirical. My own direct tests of truth are of course thus limited to my own experience. I find my own ideas true just in so far as I find them guiding me to the experience that I want to get. But of course, as my colleague constantly insists, we give credit, as social beings, to one another's verifications. Hence I regard as true many ideas that I personally have not followed out to any adequately experienced consequences. The "overwhelmingly large" number of the ideas

by which we live, "we let pass for true without attempting to verify." We do this, says
Professor James, "because it *works* to do so,
everything we know conspiring with the belief,
and nothing interfering." That is, we regard
as true those ideas which we personally find it
convenient, successful, expedient to treat as
verifiable, even though we never verify them.
The warrant of these unverifiable truths is,
however, once more, the empirical usefulness
of living as if they were verifiable. "Truth
lives," says Professor James, "for the most
part on a credit system. . . . But this all
points to direct face-to-face verification some-
where, without which the fabric of truth col-
lapses like a financial system with no cash
basis whatever. You accept my verification
of one thing, I yours of another. We trade
on each other's truth. But beliefs verified
concretely by *somebody* are the posts of the
whole superstructure." The indirectly verifiable ideas, that is, the ideas which somebody else verifies, or even those which nobody
yet verifies, but which agree sufficiently with

verified ideas, we accept because it is advantageous to accept them. It is the same thing, then, to say that an idea is true because it is useful and to say that it is useful because it is true.

Agreement with reality thus turns out, as my colleague insists, "to be an affair of leading, — leading that is useful because it is into quarters that contain objects that are important." And my colleague's account of truth culminates in these notable expressions: "'The true,' to put it very briefly, is only the expedient in the way of our thinking, just as 'the right' is only the expedient in the way of our behaving." "Pragmatism faces forward towards the future." That is, an idea is true by virtue of its expedient outcome. "It pays for our ideas to be validated, verified. Our obligation to seek truth is part of our general obligation to do what pays. The payment true ideas bring are the sole why of our duty to follow them."

The sum and substance of this theory of truth, as you see, is that the truth of an idea is determined by its "success" in yielding what my colleague frequently calls "the cash values in terms of experience," which appear as consequences of holding this idea. These values may either take the form of direct verifications in terms of sensible facts, as when one finds one's way out of the woods and sees one's home; or else the form of practically satisfying and expedient beliefs, which clash with no sensible experience, and which are personally acceptable to those who hold them. It is "expedient" to connect the latter beliefs with sensible cash values when you can. If you cannot turn them into such cash, you are at liberty to hold them, but with the conviction that, after all, the personally expedient is the true.

In any case, as you see, whatever else truth is, it is nothing static. It changes with the expediencies of your experience. And therefore those who conceive the realm of truth as essentially eternal are the objects of my colleague's most charming philosophical fury.

IV

We have, then, an authoritative exposition of pragmatism before us. You must see that this doctrine, whether it be a true doctrine, or whether it be indeed simply for some people an expedient doctrine, is certainly one that concerns our philosophy of loyalty, now that indeed we have reached the place where the relation between loyalty and truth has become, for us, a critically important relation. May we venture to ask ourselves, then: Is this pragmatism a fair expression of what we mean by truth?

In reply let me at once point out the extent to which I personally agree with my colleague, and accept his theory of truth. I fully agree with him that whenever a man asserts a truth, his assertion is a deed, — a practical attitude, an active acknowledgment of some fact. I fully agree that the effort to verify this acknowledgment by one's own personal experience, and the attempt to find truth in the form of a practical congruity between our assertions and our attained empirical results, is an effort which in our individual lives inevitably accompanies and sustains our every undertaking in the cause of truth seeking. Modern pragmatism is not indeed as original as it seems to suppose itself to be in emphasizing such views. The whole history of modern idealism is full of such assertions. I myself, as a teacher of philosophy, have for years insisted upon viewing truth in this practical way. I must joyously confess to you that I was first taught to view the nature of truth in this way when I was a young student of philosophy; and I was taught this by several great masters of modern thought. These masters were Kant, Fichte, Hegel, and Professor James himself, whose lectures, as I heard them in my youth at the Johns Hopkins University, and whose beautiful conversations and letters in later years, inspired me with an insight that helped me, rather against his own advice, to read my German idealists aright, and to see what is, after all, the eternal truth beneath all this pragmatism. For Professor James's pragmatism, despite its entertaining expressions of horror of the eternal, actually does state one aspect of eternal truth. It is, namely, eternally true that all search for truth is a practical activity, with an ethical purpose, and that a purely theoretical truth, such as should guide no significant active process, is a barren absurdity. This, however, is so far precisely what Fichte spent his life in teaching. Professor James taught me, as a student, much the same lesson; and I equally prize and honor all of my masters for that lesson; and I have been trying to live up to it ever since I first began to study the nature of truth.

So far, then, I am a pragmatist. And I also fully agree that, if we ever get truth, the attainment of truth means a living and practical success in those active undertakings in terms of which we have been trying to assert and to verify our truth. I doubt not that to say, "This is true," is the same as to say: "The ideas by means of which I define this truth are the practically and genuinely successful ideas, the ideas such that, when I follow them, I really fulfil my deepest needs." All this I not only admit; but I earnestly insist that truth is an ethical concept; and I thank from my heart the great pragmatist who so fascinated his audience last year in this place; I thank him that he taught them what, in my youth, he helped to teach me, namely, that winning the truth means winning the success which we need, and for which the whole practical nature of our common humanity continually groans and travails together in pain until now.

And yet, and yet all this still leaves open one great question. When we seek truth, we indeed seek successful ideas. But what, in Heaven's name, constitutes success? Truth-seeking is indeed a practical endeavor. But what, in the name of all the loyal, is the goal of human endeavor? Truth is a living thing. We want leading and guidance. "Lead, kindly light," — thus we address the truth. We are lost in the woods of time.

We want the way, the truth, and the life. For nothing else does all our science and our common sense strive. But what is it to have genuine abundance of life? For what do we live?

V

Here our entire philosophy of loyalty, so far as it has yet been developed, comes to our aid. The loyal, as we have said, are the only human beings who can have any reasonable hope of genuine success. If they do not succeed, then nobody succeeds. And of course the loyal do indeed live with a constant, although not with an exclusive, reference to their own personal experience and to that of other individual men. They feel their present fascination for their cause. It thrills through them. Their loyalty has, even for them, in their individual capacity what Professor James calls a cash value. And of course they like to have their friends share such cash values. Yet I ask you: Are the loyal seeking *only* the mere collection of their private experiences of their personal thrills of fascination? If you hear loyal men say: "We are in this business just for what we as individuals —we and our individual fellows — can get out of it," do you regard that way of speech as an adequate expression of their really loyal spirit? When Arnold von Winkelried rushed on the Austrian spears, did he naturally say: "Look you, my friends, I seek, in experiential terms, the cash value of my devotion; see me draw the cash." My colleague would of course retort that the hero in question, according to the legend, said, as he died: "Make way for liberty." He therefore wanted liberty, as one may insist, to get these cash values. Yes, but liberty was no individual man, and no mere heap of individual men. Liberty was a cause, a certain superhuman unity of the ideal life of a free community. It was indeed expedient that one man should die for the people. But the people also was an *unio mystica* of many in one. For that cause the hero died. And no man has ever yet experienced, in his private and individual life, the whole true cash value of that higher unity. Nor will all the individual Swiss patriots, past, present, or future, viewed as a mere collection of creatures of a day, ever draw the cash in question. If the cause exists, the treasure exists, and is indeed a cash value upon a level higher than that of our passing human life. But loyalty does not live by selling its goods for present cash in the temple of its cause. Such pragmatism it drives out of the temple. It serves, and worships, and says to the cause: "Be thine the glory."

Loyalty, then, seeks success and from moment to moment indeed thrills with a purely fragmentary and temporary joy in its love of its service. But the joy depends on a belief in a distinctly superhuman type of unity of life. And so you indeed cannot express the value of your loyalty by pointing at the mere heap of the joyous thrills of the various loyal individuals. The loyal serve a real whole of life, an experiential value too rich for any expression in merely momentary terms.

Now, is it not very much so with our love of

any kind of truth? Of course, we mortals seek for whatever verification of our truths we can get in the form of present success. But can you express our human definition of truth in terms of any collection of our human experiences of personal expediency?

Well, as to our concept of truth, let us consider a test case by way of helping ourselves to answer this question. Let us suppose that a witness appears, upon some witness-stand, and objects to taking the ordinary oath, because he has conscientious scruples, due to the fact that he is a recent pragmatist, who has a fine new definition of truth, in terms of which alone he can be sworn. Let us suppose him, hereupon, to be granted entire liberty to express his oath in his own way. Let him accordingly say, using, with technical scrupulosity, my colleague's definition of truth: "I promise to tell whatever is expedient and nothing but what is expedient, so help me future experience." I ask you: Do you think that this witness has expressed, with adequacy, that view of the nature of truth that you really wish a witness to have in mind? Of course, if he were a typical pragmatist, you would indeed be delighted to hear his testimony on the witness-stand or anywhere else. But would you accept his formula?

But let me be more precise as to the topic of this witness's possible testimony. I will use for the purpose Kant's famous case. Somebody, now dead, let us suppose, has actually left with the witness a sum of money as a wholly secret deposit to be some time returned. No written record was made of the transaction. No evidence exists that can in future be used to refute the witness if he denies the transaction and keeps the money. The questions to be asked of the witness relate, amongst other things, to whatever it may be that he believes himself to know about the estate of the deceased. I now ask, not what his duty is, but simply what it is that he rationally means to do in case he really intends to tell the truth about that deposit. Does he take merely the "forward-looking" attitude of my colleague's pragmatism? Does he mean merely to predict, as expedient, certain consequences which he expects to result either to himself or to the heirs of the estate? Of course his testimony will have consequences. But is it these which he is trying to predict? Are they his true object? Or does the truth of his statement mean the same as the expediency, either to himself or to the heirs, of any consequences whatever which may follow from his statement? Does the truth of his statement about the deposit even mean the merely present empirical fact that he now feels a belief in this statement or that he finds it just now congruent with the empirical sequences of his present memories? No, for the witness is not trying merely to tell how he feels. He is trying to tell the truth about the deposit. And the witness's belief is not the truth of his belief. Even his memory is not the truth to which he means to be a witness. And the future consequences of his making a true statement are for the witness irrelevant, since they are for the law and the heirs to determine. Yet one means something perfectly definite by the truth of the testimony of that witness. And that truth is simply inexpressible in such terms as those which my colleague employs. Yet the truth here in question is a simple truth about the witness's own personal past experience.

Now, such a case is only one of countless cases where we are trying to tell the truth about something which we all regard as being, in itself, a matter of genuine and concrete experience, while nevertheless we do not mean, "It is expedient just now for me to think this," nor yet, "I predict such and such consequences for my own personal experience, or for the future experience of some other individual man; and these predicted consequences constitute the truth of my present assertion." I say there are countless such cases where the truth that we mean is empirical indeed, but transcends all such expediencies and personal consequences. The very assertion, "Human experience, taken as a totality of facts, exists," is a momentous example of just such an assertion. We all believe that assertion. If that assertion is not actually true, then our whole frame of natural science, founded as it is on the common experience of many observers, crumbles into dust, our common sense world is nothing, business and society are alike illusions, loyalty to causes is meaningless. Now that assertion, "Human experience, that is, the totality of the experiences of many men, really exists," is an assertion which you and I regard as perfectly true. Yet no individual man ever has verified, or ever will verify, that assertion. For no man, taken as this individual man, experiences the experience of anybody but himself. Yet we all regard that assertion as true.

My colleague, of course, would say, as in fact he has often said, that his assertion is one of the numerous instances of that process of trading on credit which he so freely illustrates. We do not verify this assertion. But we accept it on credit as verifiable. However, the credit simile is a dangerous one here, so long as one conceives that the verification which would pay the cash would be a payment in the form of such human experience as you and I possess. For the assertion, "The experience of many men exists," is an assertion that is essentially unverifiable by any one man. If the "cash value" of the assertion means, then, its verifiability by any man, then the credit in question is one that simply cannot be turned into such cash by any conceivable process, occurring in our individual lives, since the very idea of the real existence of the experience of many men excludes, by its definition, the direct presence of this experience of various men within the experience of any one of these men. The credit value in question would thus be a *mere* fiat value, so long as the only cash values are those of the experiences of individual men, and the truth of our assertion would mean simply that we find it expedient to treat as verifiable what we know cannot be verified. Hereupon, of course, we should simply be trading upon currency that has no cash value. Whoever does verify the fact that the experience of many men exists, if such a verifier there be, is a superhuman being, an union of the empirical lives

of many men in the complex of a single experience. And if our credit of the assertion that
many men exist is convertible into cash at all,
that cash is not laid up where the moth and
rust of our private human experience doth from
moment to moment corrupt the very data that
we see; but is laid up in a realm where our
experiences, past, present, future, are the object of a conspectus that is not merely temporal
and transient. Now all the natural sciences
make use of the persuasion that the experiences
of various men exist, and that there is a unity
of such experiences. This thesis, then, is no
invention of philosophers.

My colleague, in answer, would of course
insist that as a fact you and I are now believing
that many men exist, and that human experience in its entirety exists, *merely* because, in the
long run, we find that this belief is indeed
congruous with our current and purely personal experience, and is therefore an expedient idea of ours. But I, in answer, insist that
common sense well feels this belief to be indeed
from moment to moment expedient, and yet

clearly distinguishes between that expediency
and the truth which common sense all the while
attributes to the belief. The distinction is precisely the one which my fancied illustration of
the pragmatist on the witness-stand has suggested. It is a perfectly universal distinction
and a commonplace one. Tell me, "This
opinion is true," and whatever you are talking
about I may agree or disagree or doubt; yet
in any case you have stated a momentous issue.
But tell me, "I just now find this belief
expedient, it feels to me congruous" and you
have explicitly given me just a scrap of your
personal biography, and have told me no other
truth whatever than a truth about the present
state of your feelings.

If, however, you emphasize my colleague's
wording to the effect that a truth is such because
it proves to be an idea that is expedient "in
the long run," I once more ask you: *When*
does a man experience the whole of the real
facts about the "long run"? At the beginning of the long run, when the end is not yet,
or at the end, when, perhaps, he forgets, like

many older men, what were once the expediencies of his youth? What decides the truth about the long run? My exalted moments, when anything that I like seems true, or my disappointed moments, when I declare that I have always had bad luck? To appeal to the genuinely real "long run" is only to appeal in still another form to a certain ideally fair conspectus of my own whole life, — a conspectus which I, in my private human experience, never get. Whoever gets the conspectus of my whole life, to see what, in the long run, is indeed for me expedient, — whoever, I say, gets that conspectus, if such a being there indeed is, — is essentially superhuman in his type of consciousness. For he sees what I only get in the form of an idea; namely, the true sense and meaning of my life.

In vain, then, does one try adequately to define the whole of what we mean by truth either in terms of our human feelings of expediency or in terms of our instantaneous thrills of joy in success, or in terms of any other verifications that crumble as the instant flies. All such verifications we use, just as we use whatever perishes. Any such object is a fragment, but we want the whole. Truth is itself a cause, and is largely as one must admit, for us mortals, just now, what we called, in our last lecture, a lost cause — else how should these pragmatists be able thus to imagine a vain thing, and call that truth which is but the crumbling expediency of the moment? Our search for truth is indeed a practical process. The attainment of truth means success. Our verifications, so far as we ever get them, are momentary fragments of that success. But the genuine success that we demand is an ethical success, of precisely the type which all the loyal seek, when they rejoice in giving all for their cause.

VI

But you will now all the more eagerly demand in what sense we can ever get any warrant for saying that we know any truth whatever. In seeking truth we do not seek the mere crumbling successes of the passing instants of human life. We seek a city out of sight.

What we get of success within our passing experience is rationally as precious to us as it is, just because we believe that attainment to be a fragment of an essentially superhuman success, which is won in the form of a higher experience than ours, — a conspectus wherein our human experiences are unified. But what warrant have we for this belief?

I will tell you how I view the case. We need unity of life. In recognizing that need my own pragmatism consists. Now, we never find unity present to our human experience in more than a fragmentary shape. We get hints of higher unity. But only the fragmentary unity is won at any moment of our lives. We therefore form ideas — very fallible ideas — of some unity of experience, an unity such as our idea of any science or any art or any united people or of any community or of any other cause, any other union of many human experiences in one, defines. Now, if our ideas are in any case indeed true, then such an unity is as a fact successfully experienced upon some higher level than ours, and is experienced in some conspectus of life which wins what we need, which approves our loyalty, which fulfils our rational will, and which has in its wholeness what we seek. And then we ourselves with all our ideas and strivings are in and of this higher unity of life. Our loyalty to truth is a hint of this unity. Our transient successes are fragments of the true success. But suppose our ideas about the structure of this higher unity to be false in any of their details. Suppose, namely, any of our causes to be wrongly viewed by us. Then there is still real that state of facts, whatever it is, which, if just now known to us, would show us this falsity of our various special ideas. Now, only an experience, a consciousness of some system of contents, could show the falsity of any idea. Hence this real state of facts, this constitution of the genuine universe, whatever it is, must again be a reality precisely in so far as it is also a conspectus of facts of experience.

We therefore already possess at least one true idea, precisely in so far as we say: "The facts of the world are what they are; the real universe exposes our errors and makes them errors." And when we say this, we once more appeal to a conspectus of experience in which ours is included. For I am in error only in case my present ideas about the true facts of the whole world of experience are out of concord with the very meaning that I myself actively try to assign to these ideas. My ideas are in any detail false, only if the very experience to which I mean to appeal, contains in its conspectus contents which I just now imperfectly conceive. In any case, then, the truth is possessed by precisely that whole of experience which I never get, but to which my colleague also inevitably appeals when he talks of the "long run," or of the experiences of humanity in general.

Whatever the truth, then, or the falsity of any of my special convictions about this or that fact may be, the real world, which refutes my false present ideas in so far as they clash with its wholeness, and which confirms them just in so far as they succeed in having significant relations to its unity,—this real world, I say, is a conspectus of the whole of experience. And this whole of experience is in the closest real relation to my practical life, precisely in so far as, for me, the purpose of my life is to get into unity with the whole universe, and precisely in so far as the universe itself is just that conspectus of experience that we all mean to define and to serve whatever we do, or whatever we say.

But the real whole conspectus of experience, the real view of the totality of life, the real expression of that will to live in and for the whole, which every assertion of truth and every loyal deed expresses — well, it must be a conspectus that includes whatever facts are indeed facts, be they past, present, or future. I call this whole of experience an eternal truth. I do not thereby mean, as my colleague seems to imagine, that the eternal first exists, and that then our life in time comes and copies that eternal order. I mean simply that the whole of experience includes all temporal happenings, contains within itself all changes, and, since it is the one whole that we all want and need, succeeds in so far as it supplements all failures, accepts all, even the blindest of services, and wins what we seek. Thus winning it is practically good and worthy.

But if one insists, How do you know all this? I reply: I know simply that to try to deny the reality of this whole of truth is simply to reaffirm it. Any special idea of mine may be wrong, even as any loyal deed may fail, or as any cause may become, to human vision, a lost cause. But to deny that there is truth, or that there is a real world, is simply to say that the whole truth is that there is no whole truth, and that the real fact is that there is no fact real at all. Such assertions are plain self-contradictions. And on the other hand, by the term "real world," defined as it is for us by our ideal needs, we mean simply that whole of experience in which we live, and in unity with which we alone succeed.

Loyalty, then, has its own metaphysic. This metaphysic is expressed in a view of things which conceives our experience as bound up in a real unity with all experience, — an unity which is essentially good, and in which all our ideas possess their real fulfilment and success. Such a view is true, simply because if you deny its truth you reaffirm that very truth under a new form.

Truth, meanwhile, means, as pragmatism asserts, the fulfilment of a need. But we all need the superhuman, the city out of sight, the union with all life, — the essentially eternal. This need is no invention of the philosophers. It is the need which all the loyal feel, whether they know it or not, and whether they call themselves pragmatists or not. To define this need as pragmatism in its recent forms has done, to reduce truth to expediency, is to go about crying *cash, cash,* in a realm where there is no cash of the sort that loyalty demands, that every scientific inquiry presupposes, and that only the unity of the experiences of many in one furnishes.

If we must, then, conceive recent pragmatism under the figure of a business enterprise, — a metaphor which my colleague's phraseology so insistently invites, — I am constrained therefore to sum up its position thus: First, with a winning clearness, and with a most honorable frankness it confesses bankruptcy, so far as the actually needed cash payments of significant truth are concerned. Secondly, it nevertheless declines to go into the hands of any real receiver, for it is not fond of anything that appears too absolute. And thirdly, it proposes simply and openly to go on doing business under the old style and title of the truth. "After all," it says, "are we not, every one of us, fond of credit values?"

But I cannot conceive the position of the loyal to be, in fact, so hopelessly embarrassed as this. The recent pragmatists themselves are, in fact, practically considered very loyal lovers of genuine truth. They simply have mistaken the true state of their accounts. We all know, indeed, little enough. But the loyal man, I think, whether he imagines himself to be a recent pragmatist or not, has a rational right to say this: My cause partakes of the nature of the only truth and reality that there is. My life is an effort to manifest such eternal truth, as well as I can, in a series of temporal deeds. I may serve my cause ill. I may conceive it erroneously. I may lose it in the thicket of this world of transient experience. My every human deed may involve a blunder. My mortal life may seem one long series of failures. But I know that my cause liveth. My true life is hid with the cause and belongs to the eternal.

VIII

LOYALTY AND RELIGION

LECTURE VIII

LOYALTY AND RELIGION

WE began these lectures with a confessedly inadequate definition of loyalty. At the last time we laid a basis for a new definition of loyalty. In this concluding lecture, we are to develop that definition, and to draw conclusions regarding the relation of loyalty to religion. Both enterprises will require a further development of our theory of truth.

I

Loyalty, so we said at the outset, is the willing and thoroughgoing devotion of a person to a cause. We defined a cause as something that unifies many human lives in one. Our intent in making these definitions was mainly practical. Our philosophy of loyalty was and is intended to be a practical philosophy. We used our definition first to help us to find out the purpose of life, and the supreme good which human beings can seek for themselves. We found this good to be, indeed, of a paradoxical seeming. It was a good found only by an act of sacrifice. We then developed the conception of loyalty to loyalty, and learned that, with this means of defining the one cause which is worthy of all men's devotion, we could unify and simplify the chaotic code of our conventional morality, could do full justice to the demands of a rational ethical individualism, and could leave to every man his right and his duty to choose some special personal cause of his own, while we could yet state the ideal of a harmony of all human causes in one all-embracing cause. Upon this basis we also could form a theory of conscience, — a theory which views conscience at once as rational and universal in its authority, and yet as individual in its expression in the life of each man, so that every man's conscience remains his own, and is, to himself, in many ways, mysterious; while the whole business of any man's conscience is, nevertheless, to direct that man to find his individual place in the one, universal, rational, moral order.

Hereupon we illustrated our theory of loyalty by applying it to a study of some of our own national problems. And next, our account of the practice of loyalty culminated in a doctrine of the nature of training for loyalty. Here we found the great paradox of loyalty afresh illustrated. Loyalty wins not only by sacrifice, but also by painful labor, and by the very agony of defeat. In this our human world the lost causes have proved themselves, in history, to be the most fruitful causes. In sum, loyalty is trained both through the presence of personal leaders, and through that idealization of our causes which adversity nourishes, which death illumines, and which the defeats of present time may render all the clearer and more ideally fascinating.

All these results showed us that loyalty has about it a character such as forbids us, after all, to interpret the true good of loyalty in terms of our merely individual human experiences. Man discovers, indeed, even within the limits of his own personal experience, that loyalty is his ethical destiny, and that without it he can win no peace; while, with loyalty once in possession of his active powers, he seems to himself to have solved the personal problem of the purpose of his life. But loyalty thus appears, after all, in the individual life, in a deeply mysterious form. It says to a man: "Your true good can never be won and verified by you in terms to which the present form and scope of our human experience is adequate. The best that you can get lies in self-surrender, and in your personal assurance that the cause to which you surrender yourself is indeed good. But your cause, if it is indeed a reality, has a good about it which no one man, and no mere collection of men, can ever verify. This good of the cause is essentially superhuman in its type, even while it is human in its embodiment. For it belongs to an union of men, to a whole of human life which transcends the individuality of any man, and which is not to be found as something belonging to any mere collection of men. Let your supreme good, then, be this, that you regard the cause as real, as good, and that, if the cause be lost to any merely human sight, you hold it to be nevertheless living in its own realm,—not apart, indeed, from human life, but in the form of the fulfilment of many human lives in one."

Now, this mysterious speech of loyalty implies something which is not only moral, but also metaphysical. Purely practical considerations, then, a study of our human needs, an ideal of the business of life, — these inevitably lead us into a region which is more than merely a realm of moral activities. This region is either one of delusions or else one of spiritual realities of a level higher than is that of our present individual human experience.

In the last lecture we undertook to consider this larger realm of spiritual unities which must be real in case our loyalty is not based upon illusion. And we attempted to sketch a general theory of truth which might show us that such spiritual unities are indeed realities, and are presupposed by our every effort to define truth. Thus our ethical theory has transformed itself into a general philosophical doctrine; and loyalty now appears to us not only as a guide of life but as a revelation of our relation to a realm which we have been obliged to define as one of an eternal and all-embracing unity of spiritual life.

We have called this realm of true life, and of genuine and united experience, — this realm which, if our argument at the last time was sound, includes our lives in that very whole which constitutes the real universe, — we have called this realm, I say, an eternal world, — eternal, simply because, according to our theory, it includes all temporal happenings and strivings in the conspectus of a single consciousness, and fulfils all our rational purposes together, and is all that we seek to be. For, as we argued, this realm of reality is conscious, is united, is self-possessed, and is perfected through the very wealth of the ideal sacrifices and of the loyal devotion which are united so as to constitute its fulness of being. In view of the philosophy that was thus sketched, I now propose a new definition of loyalty; and I say that this definition results from all of our previous study: *Loyalty is the will to manifest, so far as is possible, the Eternal, that is, the conscious and superhuman unity of life, in the form of the acts of an individual Self.* Or, if you prefer to take the point of view of an individual human self, if you persist in looking at the world just as we find it in our ordinary experience, and if you regard the metaphysical doctrine just sketched merely as an ideal theory of life, and *not* as a demonstrable philosophy, I can still hold to my definition of loyalty by borrowing a famous phrase from the dear friend and colleague some of whose views I at the last time opposed. I can, then, simply state my new definition of loyalty in plainer and more directly obvious terms thus: *Loyalty is the Will to Believe in something eternal, and to express that belief in the practical life of a human being.*

This, I say, is my new definition of loyalty, and in its metaphysical form, it is my final definition. Let me expound it further, and let me show a little more in detail how it results from the whole course of our inquiry.

II

However kindly you may have followed the discussion of my last lecture, some of you will feel doubts as to the theory of truth and of reality which I opposed to the doctrines of recent pragmatism, and which I now lay at the basis of my final definition of loyalty. I approached my own theory by the way of a polemic against my colleague's recently stated views regarding the nature of truth. But polemic often hinders our appreciation of some aspects of the questions at issue, even while it may help us to emphasize others. So let me now point out, apart from a polemic against other theories of truth, what is my main motive for viewing the real world as I do, and why I suppose that viewing the world as I do helps us to understand better the business of loyalty.

People who have faith in this or in that form of superhuman and significant reality often ask what they can do to turn their faith into something that more resembles clear insight. Shall they look into the evidences that are adduced in favor of this or of that miraculous story? Shall they themselves seek for the miraculous in their own personal experience? Will psychical research throw any light on the mysteries of being? Or, perhaps, will some sort of special mystical training reveal the higher truth? What is the way that leads towards the spiritual world? And thus those who doubt whether there are such higher realities to be found still sometimes try to get rid of these doubts by various appeals either to more or less magical arts, or to extraordinary personal experiences, or to mystical transformations of their personal life.

Now, whatever may be said of wonders, or of mystical revelations, our philosophy of loyalty is naturally interested in pointing out a road to the spiritual world, if, indeed, there be such a world, — a road, I say, which has a plain relation to our everyday moral life. And it seems to me, both that there is a genuinely spiritual world, and that there is a path of inquiry which can lead from such a practical faith in the higher world as loyalty embodies in its deeds, to a rational insight into the general constitution of this higher realm. I do not offer my opinions upon this subject as having any authority. I can see no farther through stone walls than can my fellow, and I enjoy no special revelations from any superhuman realm. But I ask you, as thoughtful people, to consider what your ordinary life, as rational beings, implies as its basis and as its truth.

What I was expounding at the close of my last lecture was a view of things which seems to me to be implied in any attempt to express, in a reasonable way, where we stand in our universe.

We all of us have to admit, I think, that our daily life depends upon believing in realities which are, in any case, just as truly beyond the scope of our ordinary individual experience as any spiritual realm could possibly be. We live by believing in one another's minds as realities. We give credit to countless reports, documents, and other evidences of present and past facts; and we do all this, knowing that such credit cannot be adequately verified by any experience such as an individual man can obtain. Now, the usual traditional account of all these beliefs of ours is that they are forced upon us, by some reality which is, as people say, wholly independent of our knowledge, which exists by itself apart from our experience, and which may be, therefore, entirely alien in its nature to any of our human interests and ideals.

But modern philosophy, — a philosophy in whose historical course of development our recent pragmatism is only a passing incident, — that philosophy which turns upon analyzing the bases of our knowledge, and upon reflectively considering what our human beliefs and ideas are intended to mean and to accomplish, has taught us to see that we can never deal with any wholly independent reality. The recent pragmatists, as I understand them, are here in full and conscious agreement with my own opinion. We can deal with no world which is out of relation to our experience. On the contrary, the real world is known to us in terms of *our* experience, is defined for us by *our* ideas, and is the object of *our* practical endeavors. Meanwhile, to declare anything real is to assert that it has its place in some realm of experience, be this experience human or superhuman. To declare that anything whatever is a fact, is simply to assert that some proposition, which you or I or some other thinking being can express in the form of intelligible ideas, is a true proposition. And the truth of propositions itself is nothing dead, is nothing independent of ideas and of experience, but is simply the successful fulfilment of some demand, — a demand which you can express in the form of an assertion, and which is fulfilled in so far, and only in so far, as some region of live experience contains what meets that demand. Meanwhile, every proposition, every assertion that anybody can make, is a deed; and every rational deed involves, in effect, an assertion of a fact. If the prodigal son says, "I will arise and go to my father," he even thereby asserts something to be. true about himself, his father, and his father's house. If an astronomer or a chemist or a statistician or a man of business reports "this or this is a fact," he even thereby performs a deed, — an act having an ideal meaning, and embodying a live purpose; and he further declares that the constitution of experience is such as to make this deed essentially reasonable, successful, and worthy to be accepted by every man.

The real world is therefore *not* something independent of us. It is a world whose stuff, so to speak, —whose content, — is of the nature of experience, whose structure meets, validates, and gives warrant to our active deeds, and whose whole nature is such that it can be interpreted in terms of ideas, propositions, and conscious meanings, while in turn it gives to our fragmentary ideas and to our conscious life whatever connected meaning they possess. Whenever I have purposes and fail, so far, to carry them out, that is because I have not yet found the true way of expressing my own relation to reality. On the other hand, precisely in so far as I have understood some whole of reality, I have carried out successfully some purpose of mine.

There is, then, no merely theoretical truth, and there is no reality foreign, in its nature, to experience. Whoever actually lives the whole conscious life such as *can* be lived out with a definitely reasonable meaning, — such a being, obviously superhuman in his grade of consciousness, not only knows the real world, but *is* the real world. Whoever is conscious of the whole content of experience possesses all reality. And our search for reality is simply an effort to discover what the whole fabric of experience is into which our human experience is woven, what the system of truth is in which our partial truths have their place, what the ideally significant life is for the sake of which every deed of ours is undertaken. When we try to find out what the real world is, we are simply trying to discover the sense of our own individual lives. And we can define that sense of our lives only in terms of a conscious life in which ours is included, in which our ideas get their full meaning expressed, and in which what we fail to carry out to the full is carried out to the full.

III

Otherwise stated, when I think of the whole world of facts, — the "real world," — I inevitably think of something that is *my own* world, precisely in so far as that world is any object of any reasonable idea of mine. It is true, of course, that, in forming an idea of my world of facts, I do not thereby give myself, at this instant, the least right to spin out of my inner consciousness any adequate present ideas of the detail of the contents of my real world. In thinking of the real world, I am indeed thinking of the whole of that very system of experience in which my experience is bound up; and in which I, as an individual, have my very limited and narrow place. But just now I am not in possession of that whole. I have to work for it and wait for it, and faithfully to be true to it. As a creature living along, from moment to moment, in time, I therefore indeed have to wait ignorantly enough for coming experience. I have to use as I can my fallible memory in trying to find out about my own past experience. I have no way of verifying what your experience is, except by using tests — and again the extremely fallible tests — which we all employ in our social life. I need the methods of the sciences of experience to guide me in the study of whatever facts fall within their scope. I use those practical and momentary successes upon which recent pragmatism insists, whenever I try to get a concrete verification of my opinions. And so far I stand, and must rightly stand, exactly where any man of common sense, any student of a science, any plain man, or any learned man stands. I am a fallible mortal, simply trying to find my way as I can in the thickets of experience.

And yet all this my daily life, my poor efforts to remember and to predict, my fragmentary inquiries into this or that matter of science or of business, my practical acknowledgment of your presence as real facts in the real world of experience, my personal definition of the causes to which I devote myself, — these are all undertakings that are overruled, and that are rendered significant, simply in so far as they are reasonable parts of one all-embracing enterprise. This enterprise is my active attempt to find out my true place in the real world. But now I can only define my real world by conceiving it in terms of experience. I can find my place in the world only by discovering where I stand in the whole system of experience. For what I mean by a fact is something that somebody finds. Even a merely possible fact is something only in so far as somebody actually *could* find it. And the sense in which it *is* an actual fact that somebody *could* find in his experience a determinate fact, is a sense which again can only be defined in terms of concrete, living, and not merely possible experience, and in terms of some will or purpose expressed in a conscious life. Even possible facts, then, are *really* possible only in so far as something is actually experienced, or is found by somebody. Whatever is real, then, be it distant or near, past or future, present to your mind or to mine, a physical fact or a moral fact, a fact of our possible human experience, or a fact of a superhuman type of experience, a purpose, a desire, a natural object or an ideal object, a mechanical system or a value, — whatever, I say, is real, *is real as a content present to some conscious being.* Therefore, when I inquire about the real world, I am simply asking what contents of experience, human or superhuman, are actually and consciously found by somebody. My inquiries regarding facts, of whatever grade the facts may be, are therefore inevitably an effort to find out *what the world's experience is.* In all my common sense, then, in all my science, in all my social life, I am trying to discover what the universal conscious life which constitutes the world contains as its contents, and views as its own.

But even this is not the entire story of my place in the real world. For I cannot inquire about facts without forming my own ideas of these facts. In so far as my ideas are true, my own personal ideas are therefore active processes that go on within the conscious life of the world. If my ideas are true, they succeed in agreeing with the very world consciousness that they define. But this agreement, this success, if itself it is a fact at all, is once more a fact of experience, — yet not merely of my private experience, since I myself never personally find, within the limits of my own individual experience, the success that every act of truth seeking demands. If I get the truth, then, at any point of my life, my success is real only in so far as some conscious life, which includes my ideas and my efforts, and which also includes the very facts of the world whereof I am thinking, actually observes my success, in the form of a conspectus of the world's facts, and of my own efforts to find and to define them.

In so far, then, as I get the truth about the world, I myself am a fragmentary conscious life that is included within the conscious conspectus of the world's experience, and that is in one self-conscious unity with that world consciousness. And it is in this unity with the world consciousness that I get my success, and am in concord with the truth.

But of course any particular idea of mine, regarding the world, or regarding any fact in the world, may be false. However, this possibility of my error is itself a real situation of mine, and involves essentially the same relation between the world and myself which obtains in case I have true ideas. For I can be in error about an object only in case I really mean to agree with that object, and to agree with it in a way which only my own purposes, in seeking this agreement, can possibly define. It is only by virtue of my own undertakings that I can fail in my undertakings. It is only because, after all, I am loyal to the world's whole truth that I can so express myself in fallible ideas, and in fragmentary opinions that, as a fact, I may, at any moment, undertake too much for my own momentary success to be assured, so that I can indeed in any one of my assertions fail justly to accord with that world consciousness which I am all the while trying to interpret in my own transient way. But when I thus fail, I momentarily fail *to interpret my place in the very world consciousness whose life I am trying to define.* But my failure, when and in so far as it occurs, is once more a fact, — and therefore a fact for the world's consciousness. If I blunder, but am sincere, if I think myself right, but am not right, then my error is a fact for a consciousness which includes my fallible attempts to be loyal to the truth, but which sees how they just now lose present touch with their true cause. Seeing this my momentary defeat, the world consciousness sees, however, my loyalty, and in its conspectus assigns, even to my fragmentary attempts at truth, their genuine place in the single unity of the world's consciousness. My very failure, then, like every loyal failure, is still a sort of success. It is an effort to define my place in the unity of the world's conspectus of all conscious life. I cannot fall out of that unity. I cannot flee from its presence, And I err only as the loyal may give up their life for their cause. Whether I get truth, then, or whether I err in detail, *my loyal search for truth insures the fact that I am in a significant unity with the world's conscious life.*

The thesis that the world is one whole and a significant whole of conscious life is, for these reasons, a thesis which can only be viewed as an error, by reinstating this very assertion under a new form. For any error of mine concerning the world is possible only in so far as I really mean to assert the truth about the world; and this real meaning of mine can exist only as a fact within the conspectus of consciousness for which the real whole world exists, and within which I myself live.

This, then, in brief, is my own theory of truth. This is why I hold this theory to be no fantastic guess about what may be true, but a logically inevitable conclusion about how every one of us, wise or ignorant, is actually defining his own relation to truth, whether he knows the fact or not. I expressed my theory at the last time in terms of a polemic against the recent pragmatists; but as a fact their view, in its genuine and deeper meaning, is no more opposed to mine than my young Russian's vehement protest against loyalty, quoted in my second lecture, was, in its true spirit, opposed to my own view. My young Russian, you may remember, hated what he took to be loyalty, just because he was so loyal. And even so my friends, the recent pragmatists, reassert my theory of truth even in their every attempt to deny it. For, amongst other things, they assert that their own theory of truth is actually true. And that assertion implies just such a conspectus of all truth in one view, — just such a conspectus as I too assert.

IV

We first came in sight of this theory of truth, in these discussions, for a purely practical reason. Abstract and coldly intellectual as the doctrine, when stated as I have just stated it, may appear, we had our need to ask what truth is, because we wanted to know whether the loyal are right in supposing, as they inevitably do suppose, that their personal causes, and that their cause of causes, namely, universal loyalty, that any such causes, I say, possess genuine foundation in truth. Loyalty, as we found, is a practical service of superhuman objects. For our causes transcend expression in terms of our single lives. If the cause lives, then all conscious moral life—even our poor human life—is in unity with a superhuman conscious life, in which we ourselves dwell; and in this unity we win, in so far as we are loyal servants of our cause, a success which no transient human experience of ours, no joyous thrill of the flying moment, no bitterness of private defeat and loss, can do more or less than to illustrate, to illumine, or to idealize.

We asked: Is this faith of the loyal in their causes a pathetic fallacy? Our theory of truth has given us a general answer to this intensely practical question. The loyal try to live in the spirit. But, if thereupon

they merely open their eyes to the nature
of the reasonable truth, they see that it is in
the spirit only that they do or can live. They
would be living in this truth, as mere passing
fragments of conscious life, as mere blind
series of mental processes, even if they were
not loyal. For all life, however dark and fragmentary, is either a blind striving for conscious unity with the universal life of which
it is a fragment, or else, like the life of the
loyal, is a deliberate effort to express such a
striving in the form of a service of a superhuman cause. *And all lesser loyalties, and
all serving of imperfect or of evil causes, are
but fragmentary forms of the service of the
cause of universal loyalty.* To serve universal loyalty is, however, to view the interests
of all conscious life as one; and to do this is
to regard all conscious life as constituting just
such an unity as our theory of truth requires.
Meanwhile, since truth seeking is indeed itself a practical activity, what we have stated
in our theory of truth is itself but an aspect
of the very life that the loyal are leading.

Whoever seeks any truth is loyal, for he is determining his life by reference to a life which transcends his own. And he is loyal to loyalty; for whatever truth you try to discover is, if true, valid for everybody, and is therefore worthy of everybody's loyal recognition. The loyal, then, are truth seekers; and the truth seekers are loyal. And all of them live for the sake of the unity of all life. And this unity includes us all, but is superhuman.

Our view of truth, therefore, meets at once an ethical and a logical need. The real world is precisely that world in which the loyal are at home. Their loyalty is no pathetic fallacy. Their causes are real facts in the universe. The universe as a whole possesses that unity which loyalty to loyalty seeks to express in its service of the whole of life.

Herewith, however, it occurs to us to ask one final question. Is not this real world, whose true unity the loyal acknowledge by their every deed, and whose conscious unity every process of truth seeking presupposes, — is not this also the world which religion recognizes? If so, what is the relation of loyalty to religion?

The materials for answering this question are now in our hands. We have been so deliberate in preparing them for our present purpose, just for the sake of making our answer the simpler when it comes.

V

We have now defined loyalty as the will to manifest the eternal in and through the deeds of individual selves. As for religion, — in its highest historical forms (which here alone concern us), — religion, as I think, may be defined as follows. Religion (in these its highest forms) *is the interpretation both of the eternal and of the spirit of loyalty through emotion, and through a fitting activity of the imagination.*

Religion, in any form, has always been an effort to interpret and to make use of some superhuman world. The history, the genesis, the earlier and simpler forms of religion, the relations of religion and morality in the primitive life of mankind, do not here concern us. It is enough to say that, in history, there has often been a serious tension between the interests of religion and those of morality. For the higher powers have very generally seemed to man to be either non-moral or immoral. This very tension, only too frequently, still exists for many people to-day. One of the greatest and hardest discoveries of the human mind has been the discovery of how to reconcile, not religion and science, but religion and morality. Whoever knows even a small portion of the history of the cults of mankind is aware of the difficulties to which I refer. The superhuman has been conceived by men in terms that were often far enough from those which loyalty requires. Whoever will read over the recorded words of a writer nowadays too much neglected, the rugged and magnificently loyal Old Testament prophet Amos, can see for himself how bravely the difficulty of conceiving the superhuman as the righteous, was faced by one of the first who ever viewed the relation of religion and morality as our best teachers have since taught us to view them. And yet such a reader can also see how hard this very task of the prophet was. When we remember also that so great a mind as that of the originator of Buddhism, after all the long previous toil of Hindoo thought upon this great problem, could see no way to reconcile religion and morality, except by bringing them both to the shores of the mysterious and soundless ocean of Nirvana, and sinking them together in its depths (an undertaking which Buddha regarded as the salvation of the world), we get a further view of the nature of the problem. When we remember that St. Paul, after many years of lonely spiritual struggle, attempted in his teaching to reconcile morality and religion by an interpretation of Christianity which has ever since kept the Christian world in a most inspiring ferment of theological controversy and of practical conflict, we are again instructed as to the seriousness of the issue. But as a fact, the experience of the civilized man has gradually led him to see how to reconcile the moral life and the religious spirit. Since this reconciliation is one which our theory of truth, and of the constitution of the real world, substantially justifies, we are now ready for a brief review of the entire situation.

People often say that mere morality is something very remote from true religion. Sometimes people say this in the interests of religion, meaning to point out that mere morality can at best make you only a more or less tolerable citizen, while only religion can reconcile you, as such people say, to that superhuman world whose existence and whose support alone make human life worth living. But sometimes almost the same assertion is made in the interest of pure morality, viewed as something independent of religion. Some people tell you, namely, that since, as they say, religion is a collection of doubtful beliefs, of superstitions, and of more or less exalted emotions, morality is all the better for keeping aloof from religion. Suffering man needs your help; your friends need as much happiness as you can give them; conventional morality is, on the whole, a good thing. Learn righteousness, therefore, say they, and leave religion to the fantastic-minded who love to believe. The human is what we need. Let the superhuman alone.

Now, our philosophy of loyalty, aiming at something much larger and richer than the mere sum of human happiness in individual men, has taught us that there is no such sharp dividing line between the human and the superhuman as these attempts to sunder the provinces of religion and morality would imply. The loyal serve something more than individual lives. Even Nietzsche, individualist and ethical naturalist though he was, illustrates our present thesis. He began the later period of his teaching by asserting that "God is dead"; and (lest one might regard this as a mere attack upon monotheism, and might suppose Nietzsche to be an old-fashioned heathen polytheist) he added the famous remark that, in case any gods whatever existed, he could not possibly endure being himself no god. "*Therefore*," so he reasoned, "*there are no gods.*" All this seems to leave man very much to his own devices. Yet Nietzsche at once set up the cult of the ideal future being called the *Uebermensch* or Superman. And the *Uebermensch* is just as much of a god as anybody who ever throned upon Olympus or dwelt in the sky. And if the doctrine of the "Eternal Recurrence," as Nietzsche defined it, is true, the *Uebermensch* belongs not only to the ideal future, but has existed an endless number of times already.

If our philosophy of loyalty is right, Nietzsche was not wrong in this appeal to the superhuman. The superhuman we indeed have always with us. Life has no sense without it. But the superhuman need not be the magical. It need not be the object of superstition. And if we are desirous of unifying the interests of morality and religion, it is well indeed to begin, as rugged old Amos began, by first appreciating what righteousness is, and then by interpreting righteousness, in a perfectly reasonable and non-super-

stitious way, in superhuman terms. Then
we shall be ready to appreciate what religion,
whose roots are indeed by no means wholly in
our moral nature, nevertheless has to offer us
as a supplement to our morality.

VI

Loyalty is a service of causes. But, as we
saw, we do not, we cannot, wait until somebody clearly shows us how good the causes
are in themselves, before we set about serving
them. We first practically learn of the goodness of our causes through the very act of
serving them. Loyalty begins, then, in all of
us, in elemental forms. A cause fascinates
us — we at first know not clearly why. We
give ourselves willingly to that cause. Herewith our true life begins. The cause may
indeed be a bad one. But at worst it is our
way of interpreting the true cause. If we
let our loyalty develop, it tends to turn into
the service of the universal cause. Hence I
deliberately declined, in this discussion, to
base my theory of loyalty upon that meta-

physical doctrine which I postponed to my latest lectures. It is a very imperfect view of the real world which most youth get before them before they begin to be loyal. Hosts of the loyal actually manifest the eternal in their deeds, and know not that they do so. They only know that they are given over to their cause. The first good of loyalty lies, then, in the fact which we emphasized in our earlier lectures. Reverberating all through you, stirring you to your depths, loyalty first unifies your plan of life, and thereby gives you what nothing else can give, — your self as a life lived in accordance with a plan, your conscience as your plan interpreted for you through your ideal, your cause expressed as your personal purpose in living.

In so far, then, one can indeed be loyal without being consciously and explicitly religious. One's cause, in its first intention, appears to him human, concrete, practical. It is *also* an ideal. It is *also* a superhuman entity. It also really *means* the service of the eternal. But this fact may be, to the hard-working, and especially to the unimaginative, and, in a worldly sense, fairly successful man, a latent fact. He then, to be sure, gradually idealizes his cause as he goes; but this idealizing in so far becomes no very explicitly emphasized process in his life, although, as we have seen, some tendency to deify the cause is inevitable.

Meanwhile, such an imperfectly developed but loyal man may also accept, upon traditional grounds, a religion. This religion will then tell him about a superhuman world. But in so far the religion need not be, to his mind, an essential factor in his practical loyalty. He may be superstitious; or he may be a religious formalist; or he may accept his creed and his church simply because of their social respectability and usefulness; or, finally, he may even have a rich and genuine religious experience, which still may remain rather a mysticism than a morality, or an æsthetic comfort rather than a love of his cause.

In such cases, loyalty and religion may long

keep apart. But the fact remains that loyalty, if sincere, involves at least a latent belief in the superhuman reality of the cause, and means at least an unconscious devotion to the one and eternal cause. But such a belief is also a latent union of morality and religion. Such a service is an unconscious piety. The time may come, then, when the morality will consciously need this union with the religious creed of the individual whose growth we are portraying.

This union must begin to become an explicit union whenever that process which, in our sixth lecture, we called the idealizing of the cause, reaches its higher levels. We saw that those higher levels are reached in the presence of what seems to be, to human vision, a lost cause. If we believe in the lost cause, we become directly aware that we are indeed seeking a city out of sight. If such a cause is real, it belongs to a superhuman world. Now, every cause worthy, as we said, of lifelong service, and capable of unifying our life plans, shows sooner or later that it is a cause *which we cannot successfully express in any set of human experiences of transient joys and of crumbling successes.* Human life taken merely as it flows, viewed merely as it passes by in time and is gone, is indeed a lost river of experience that plunges down the mountains of youth and sinks in the deserts of age. Its significance comes solely through its relations to the air and the ocean and the great deeps of universal experience. For by such poor figures I may, in passing, symbolize that really rational relation of our personal experience to universal conscious experience, — that relation to which I have devoted these last two lectures.

Everybody ought to serve the universal cause in his own individual way. For this, as we have seen, is what loyalty, when it comes to know its own mind, really means. But whoever thus serves inevitably *loses* his cause in our poor world of human sense-experience, because his cause is too good for this present temporal world to express it. And that is, after all, what the old theology meant when it called you and me, as we now naturally are, lost beings. Our deepest loyalty lies in devoting ourselves to causes that are just now lost to our poor human nature. One can express this, of course, by saying that the true cause is indeed real enough, in the higher world, while it is our poor human nature which is lost. Both ways of viewing the case have their truth. Loyalty means a transformation of our nature.

Lost causes, then, we must serve. But as we have seen, in our sixth lecture, loyalty to a lost cause has two companions, grief and imagination. Now, these two are the parents of all the higher forms of genuinely ethical religion. If you doubt the fact, read the scriptures of any of the great ethical faiths. Consult the psalter, the hymns, the devotional books, or the prayers of the church. Such religion interprets the superhuman in forms that our longing, our grief, and our imagination invent, but also in terms that are intended to meet the demands of our highest loyalty. For we are loyal to that unity of life which, as our truer moral consciousness learns to believe, owns the whole real world, and constitutes the cause of causes. In being loyal to universal loyalty, we are serving the unity of life.

This true unity of the world-life, however, is at once very near to us and very far from us. Very near it is; for we have our being in it, and depend upon it for whatever worth we have. Apart from it we are but the gurgling stream soon to be lost in the desert. In union with it we have individual significance in and for the whole. But we are very far from it also, because our human experience throws such fragmentary light upon the details of our relation to its activities. Hence in order to feel our relations to it as vital relations, we have to bring it near to our feelings and to our imaginations. And we long and suffer the loneliness of this life as we do so. But because we know of the details of the world only through our empirical sciences, while these give us rather materials for a rational life than a view of the unity of life, we are indeed left to our imagination to assuage grief and to help in the training of loyalty. For here, that is, precisely as to the *details* of the system of facts whereby our life is linked to the eternal, our science forsakes us. We can know *that* we are thus linked. *How* we are linked, our sciences do not make manifest to us.

Hence the actual content of the higher ethical religions is endlessly rich in legend and in other symbolic portrayal. This portrayal is rich in emotional meaning and in vivid detail. What this portrayal attempts to characterize is, in its general outline, an absolute truth. This truth consists in the following facts: *First, the rational unity and goodness of the world-life; next, its true but invisible nearness to us, despite our ignorance; further, its fulness of meaning despite our barrenness of present experience; and yet more, its interest in our personal destiny as moral beings; and finally, the certainty that, through our actual human loyalty, we come, like Moses, face to face with the true will of the world, as a man speaks to his friend.* In recognizing these facts, we have before us what may be called the creed of the Absolute Religion.

You may well ask, of course, whether our theory of truth, as heretofore expounded, gives any warrant to such religious convictions. I hold that it does give warrant to them. The symbols in which these truths are expressed by one or another religion are indeed due to all sorts of historical accidents, and to the most varied play of the imaginations both of the peoples and of the religious geniuses of our race. But that our relations to the world-life are relations wherein we are consciously met, from the other side, by a superhuman and yet strictly personal conscious life, in which our own personalities are themselves bound up, but which also is not only richer but is more concrete and definitely conscious and real than we are, — this seems to me to be an inevitable corollary of my theory of truth.

VII

And now, finally, to sum up our whole doctrine of loyalty and religion. Two things belonging to the world-life we know — two at least, if my theory is true: *it is defined in terms of our own needs; and it includes and completes our experience.* Hence, in any case, it is precisely as live and elemental and concrete as we are; and there is not a need of 'ours which is not its own. If you ask why I call it good — well, the very arguments which recent pragmatism has used are, as you remember, here my warrant. A truth cannot be a merely theoretical truth. True is that which successfully fulfils an idea. Whoever, again, is not succeeding, or is facing an evil, or is dissatisfied, is inevitably demanding and defining facts that are far beyond him, and that are not yet consciously his own. A knower of the totality of truth is therefore, of necessity, in possession of the fulfilment of all rational purposes. If, however, you ask why this world-life permits any evil whatever, or any finitude, or any imperfections, I must indeed reply that here is no place for a general discussion of the whole problem of evil, which I have repeatedly and wearisomely considered in other discussions of mine. But this observation does belong here. Our theory of evil is indeed no "shallow optimism," but is founded upon the deepest, the bitterest, and the dearest moral experience of the human race. The *loyal*, and they alone, know the one great good of suffering, of ignorance, of finitude, of loss, of defeat — *and that is just the good of loyalty*, so long as the cause itself can only be viewed as indeed a living whole. Spiritual peace is surely no easy thing. We win that peace only through stress and suffering and loss and labor. But when we find the preciousness of the idealized cause emphasized through grief, we see that, whatever evil is, it at least *may* have its place in an ideal order. What would be the universe without loyalty; and what would loyalty be without trial? And when we remember that, from this point of view, our own griefs are the griefs of the very world consciousness itself, in so far as this world-life is expressed in our lives, it may well occur to us that the life of loyalty with all its griefs and burdens and cares may be the very foundation of the attainment of that spiritual triumph which we must conceive as realized by the world spirit.

Perhaps, however, one weakly says: "If the world will attains in its wholeness what we seek, why need we seek that good at all?" I answer at once that our whole philosophy of loyalty instantly shows the vanity of such speech. Of course, the world-life does *not* obtain the individual good that is involved in my willing loyalty unless indeed *I am loyal*. The cause may in some way triumph without me, but not as *my* cause. We have never defined our theory as meaning that the world-life is *first* eternally complete, but *then* asks us, in an indifferent way, to copy its perfections. Our view is that each of us who is loyal is doing his unique deed in that whole of life which we have called the eternal simply because it is the conspectus of the totality of life, past, present, and future. If my deed were not done, the world-life would miss my deed. Each of us can say that. The very basis of our theory of truth, which we found upon the deeds, the ideas, the practical needs, of each of us, gives every individual his unique place in the world order — his deed that nobody else can do, his will which is his own. "Our wills are ours to make them thine." The unity of the world is *not* an ocean in which we are lost, but a life which is and which needs all our lives in one. Our loyalty defines that unity for us as a living, active unity. We have come to the unity through the understanding of our loyalty. It is an eternal unity only in so far as it includes all time and change and life and deeds. And therefore, when we reach this view, since the view simply fulfils what loyalty demands, our loyalty remains as precious to us, and as practical, and as genuinely a service of a cause, as it was before. It is no sort of "moral holiday" that this whole world-life suggests to us. It is precisely as a whole life of ideal strivings in which we have our places as individual selves and are such selves only in so far as we strive to do our part in the whole, — it is thus, and thus only, that our philosophy of loyalty regards the universe.

Religion, therefore, precisely in so far as it attempts to conceive the universe as a conscious and personal life of superhuman meaning, and as a life that is in close touch with our own meaning, is eternally true. But now it is just this *general* view of the universe as a rational order that is indeed open to our rational knowledge. No part of such a doctrine gives us, however, the present right as human beings to determine with any certainty the details of the world-life, except in so far as they come within the scope of our scientific and of our social inquiries. Hence, when religion, in the service of loyalty, interprets the world-life to us with symbolic detail, it gives us indeed merely symbols of the eternal truth. That this truth is indeed eternal, that our loyalty brings us into personal relations with a personal world-life, which values our every loyal deed, and needs that deed, all this is true and rational. And just this is what religion rightly illustrates. But the parables, the symbols, the historical incidents that the religious imagination uses in its portrayals, — these are the more or less sacred and transient *accidents* in which the "real presence" of the divine at once shows itself to us, and hides the detail of its inner life from us. These accidents of the religious imagination endure through many ages; but they also vary from place to place and from one nation or race of men to another, and they ought to do so. Whoever sees the living truth of the personal and conscious and ethical unity of the world *through* these symbols is possessed of the absolute religion, whatever be his nominal creed or church. Whoever overemphasizes the empirical details of these symbols, and then asks us to accept these details as literally true, commits an error which seems to me simply to invert that error whereof, at the last time, I ventured to accuse my pragmatist friends. Such a literalist, who reads his symbols as revelations of the detailed structure of the divine life, seems to me, namely, to look for the eternal *within* the realm of the mere data of human sense and imagination. To do this, I think, is indeed to seek the risen Lord in the open sepulchre.

Concerning the living truth of the whole conscious universe, one can well say, as one observes the special facts of human sense and imagination: "He is not here; he is arisen." Yet equally from the whole circle of the heaven of that entire self-conscious life which *is* the truth, there comes always, and to all the loyal, the word: "Lo, I am with you always even unto the end of the world."

INDEX

ABSTRACTIONS: impersonal abstractions cannot be proper objects of loyalty, 20, 52.

AGREEMENT: with reality, in relation to truth, 316, 322, 324, 327, 328, 340–346, 360–373.

ALTRUISM: a mere fragment of goodness, 218; relations of, to benevolence, to justice, and to loyalty, see BENEVOLENCE and JUSTICE.

AMERICAN PROBLEMS: problem of family loyalty, 220–228; loyalty to the national government, 233–236; the problem of the "self-estranged social mind," 238–244; provincialism as a means of training loyalty, 245–248; defective loyalty in our national life, 217–220; defective patriotism, 233–236; holidays, 267, 268; sport, 265–267.

ANCESTRAL TENDENCIES: as basis of our conflicting natural desires, 27, 28, 31, 57.

ARISTOTLE: 26.

ARNOLD VON WINKELRIED: 113, 329.

ART AND LOYALTY: 289, 290.

AUGUSTINE, SAINT: 26.

AUTHORITY: of the moral law, dependent for its justification upon our own rational will, 25; individualistic revolt against authority, 3–6, 33–35, 37, 60, 65–67, 83, 84, 92–95; decline of family authority, 220–223; loyalty not blind submission to authority, 42, 58, 71–79, 94, 95, 110, 199, 226; authority of

conscience defined and explained, 172–179.

AUTONOMY: of the rational will, principle of, as fundamental in ethics, 24–27; paradox regarding this autonomy, 30, 31, 34–37; loyalty as the solution of the paradox, 38–42; autonomy as defined by some forms of individualism, 84, 85, 92; loyalty as the means of securing moral autonomy, 95, 110. See also SELF, SELF-WILL, and LOYALTY.

BENEVOLENCE: its relation to loyalty, and to justice, 15,.144; definition of benevolence, 145; apart from loyalty is sentimentalism, but necessarily attends loyalty, 160.

BUDDHISM: influence of, upon the Japanese ideal of loyalty, 73; relation of Buddhism to the historical conflicts between religious and moral interests, 379.

BUSHIDO: the Japanese concept of loyalty sketched, 70–76; it is not without individualistic features, 72, 73, 74, 76; is a counter-instance to urge against the partisans of false individualism, 71, 75; its training of serenity and self-control, 76; its relation to patriotism, 235.

CASH VALUE: as a metaphorical expression for the nature of truth, 321–323, 328, 329, 346, 347.

INDEX

INDEX

of ethical standards, 9–12; limitations of the study of ethics proposed in the present work, 7; a revision of ethical doctrine no mere break with the past, 11, 12; problem of ethics stated, 24–31; this problem insoluble in terms of mere convention, 33–37; loyalty as a personal solution of the problem for any given individual, 38–47; the ethics of individualism discussed, 59–98; loyalty to loyalty as a general solution of the problem of ethics, 111–128; application of this solution to the special virtues, 128–146. *See also* CONSCIENCE, DUTY, LOYALTY, MORALITY.

EVIL: problem of, 394.

EXPEDIENCY AND TRUTH: 322, 331–340.

FAIR PLAY: in sport as a form of loyalty to loyalty, 158, 163, 267.

FAMILY, THE: in modern American life, 220–228; decline of family authority, 220, 221; the family ties are opportunities for loyalty, or else forms of loyalty, 221; their value, 221–223; the preciousness of family loyalty, 223–228.

FIDELITY: to the personal cause once chosen, is an inseparable aspect of the principle of loyalty to loyalty, 157, 190–192, 207, 221, 222, 226; but is also limited in its range of application by that principle, 208; and hereby the conditions which may require the breaking of ties are defined, 157, 208, 224.

FICHTE, J. G.: 325, 326.

FORTUNE: contrast between fortune as viewed by the power-seekers and as viewed by the loyal, 87–92.

FOURTH OF JULY: 267.

FRIENDSHIP: 287.

GENEROSITY: 150, 161.

GEORGE, HENRY: 4.

GOOD, THE: is determined for each individual by his own will and desire, 25; but is yet not definable in terms of pleasure and pain, 28; nor yet in terms of happiness, 81; nor in terms of social conformity, 82–84; nor in terms of Power, 84–92; nor in terms of autonomy apart from loyalty, 93; nor in terms of serenity apart from activity, 95–97. Loyalty as a supreme good for the individual, 21–24, 39–47, 57–59, 75–77, 98, 112–114, 124, 125–152; loyalty to loyalty as an universal good, 118, 126, 127, 153–158; the good and the expedient in relation to the concept of truth, 322, 323, 328–331, 337–340; the good in its relation to the problem of evil, 392; the goodness of the world no reason for a "moral holiday," 395.

GRAY'S ELEGY: cited, 123.

GRIEF AND IMAGINATION: as the accompaniments of loyalty to lost causes, 283; consequences of this union, 281–285; relation between religion and morality thus brought to pass, 285, 286; the higher ethical religions as the products of grief and imagination, 388.

HEGEL: on the "self-estranged social mind," 238–241; on the nature of truth, 325.

HESITANCY: corrected by loyalty, 22; opposed by the decisiveness which loyalty requires, 185–196. False individualism as a form of hesitancy, 98.

HOLIDAYS: 267.

HORA NOVISSIMA: 283.

402

INDEX

IBSEN : 4, 98.

IDEALIZING OF THE CAUSE : process described and illustrated, 268 *sqq.;* relation to lost causes, 276–286, 291–298; to art and religion, 288–291; to religious truth, 386–398; to the general theory of truth and reality, LECTURES VII AND VIII.

IMAGINATION : in its influence upon the idealizing of lost causes, and upon the origin of higher religion, *see* GRIEF and IMAGINATION.

INDEPENDENCE : as an ideal of individual life, 92–95. *See* AUTONOMY, AUTHORITY, INDIVIDUALISM, and LOYALTY.

INDIVIDUALISM : as an assailant of conventional morality in recent times, 4; the ethics of individualism discussed, 59–98; four forms of individualism illustrated, 60–70; comparison of the Japanese type of loyalty with the claims of individualism, 70–76; basis and relative justification of individualism, 77–80; criticism of special individualistic ideals, 81–98; individual happiness as an ideal, 81, cf. 28–30; revolt of individualism against mere conventionality justified, 84; power as an individualistic ideal, 84–91; moral autonomy, 92–94, cf. 24–26; individual serenity, 95–97; individualism fulfilled only in loyalty, 98; loyalty as determined by individual choice, 110, 130, 133, 185–196; the reconciliation of loyalty and individualism, 199, 200, 223–228; the individual without loyalty as a "spoke out of a wheel," 222; as morally dead, 225; the moral self as defined through its cause, 171, 172.

INSTINCTS : their variety and their relation to desires, to pleasure, and to pain, 28–30. *See also* DESIRES, and PLEASURE AND PAIN.

ISRAEL : religion of, due to loyalty to a lost cause, 278, 279; consequences for Christianity and for the world, 279, 280, 293.

JAMES, PROFESSOR WILLIAM : On "The Will to Believe," 189, 357; his doctrine regarding the nature of truth expounded, 315–323; criticised, 324–340; the author's obligations to him as teacher and friend, 325–327.

JAPANESE LOYALTY : *see* BUSHIDO, 72–77.

JAPANESE PATRIOTISM : *id.,* see also 235.

JOHNS HOPKINS UNIVERSITY : 325.

JUSTICE : definition of, 144; is one aspect of loyalty, *id., see also* 15; its relation to benevolence and kindness, 145, 162.

KANT : 26, 64, 79, 325.

LABOR-UNIONS : 229–232, 244.

LEE, ROBERT E. : 183, 193.

LEGEND : in religion, 390.

LIBERTY : without loyalty is worthless to any people, 211.

LINCOLN, ABRAHAM : 212.

LOST CAUSES : their significance for the history and for the individual training of loyalty, 277–286, 291–295; for the unifying of the moral and the religious consciousness, 297, 298, 386–389.

LOVE OF MANKIND : in relation to the principle of loyalty to loyalty, 150, 159–162, 214.

LOYALTY : plan of a Philosophy of Loyalty outlined, 12–16; preliminary definition of loyalty, 16, 17, cf. also 252–254; final definition of loyalty, 357; relation of loyalty to the concept of a cause to which one is loyal, 18, 19; loyalty never a

403

INDEX

social training, 32; is in need of unified plans of life, 57–59, 123–125; and possesses an innate power to acquire a conscience, 177.

NIETZSCHE: 4, 85, 98, 381, 382.

NITOBE: 72.

OBEDIENCE: in relation to loyalty, 40, 41, 72–77, 82–84, 98, 102–106, 109, 124, 125, 220, 221.

OLD TESTAMENT: 279.

OMAR KHAYYAM: quoted, 58.

PAIN: see PLEASURE AND PAIN.

PATRIOTISM: 39–41; Japanese, 72–77, 235; lack of true patriotism in modern American life, 228–237.

PHILOSOPHY: 13.

PHILOSOPHY OF LOYALTY: use and definition of the phrase, 12–14; outline of the plan of such a philosophy, 14–16; general summary of the philosophy of loyalty, 351–358; a philosophy of loyalty must include a theory about the real universe, 301–307. See also LOYALTY, CONSCIENCE, INDIVIDUALISM, MORALITY.

PLANS OF LIFE: their social origin, and their relation to loyalty, 34, 38, 42, 57; to the definition of the Self, 167–172; to conscience, 172–179; the duty of decisiveness regarding the plans of life, 185–196.

PLATO: 26.

PLEASURE AND PAIN: in what way objects of desire, 28, 29; the art of pleasure seeking one of the hardest of arts, 30; the good not definable in terms of happiness, 81, 82; the pain of defeat as an aid in the idealizing of lost causes, 281–284, 295; the pain of labor for the cause as an aid to loyalty, 296, 297; suffering as an indis-

pensable aspect of the spiritual life, 393.

PLOTINUS: 69.

POLITICAL PARTIES IN AMERICA: 229–232.

PORTIA: 127.

POWER: doctrine that the highest good for the individual is power, stated, 84; illustrated by the thesis of Nietzsche, 85, 86; the doctrine criticised, 86–89; contrast between the search for power and the loyal service of a cause, 89–91; summary of the case against power as an ideal, 91, 92; national prowess valuable as an instrument for serving universal loyalty, 214.

PRAGMATISM: as a doctrine concerning the nature of truth, 315 sqq.; Professor William James's form of pragmatism expounded, 316–323; criticised, 324–340; in what sense the author's theory of truth is a form of pragmatism, 324–326; in what sense opposed to the doctrine of James, 327–331; the pragmatist on the witness-stand, 331; in what sense truth transcends all verifications in terms of individual human experiences, 339, 340; bankruptcy of recent pragmatism, 346, 347. See TRUTH.

PROVINCIALISM: as an antidote to the evils of the "self-estranged social mind" in America, and as a means for the teaching of loyalty, 245–248.

REALITY: the theory of truth and of reality which is needed to complete the philosophy of loyalty, 301–313; truth seeking and loyalty, 313–315; relation of this doctrine of truth and reality to pragmatism, 315–340; warrant for the

INDEX

INDEX

this view against pragmatism, 315–340; the positive warrant for viewing the union of individuals as real, 340–348, 358–376.

UNITY: of individual life, as a result of loyalty, 22, 58, 124, 133, 169–172; as related to conscience, 172–179. — The unity of various individuals in one super-individual life as demanded by the conception of a cause, 20, 307–313. See CAUSE, LOYALTY, RELIGION, and UNION.

UNIVERSE: 307. See REALITY and TRUTH.

VALUES, MORAL: they must be estimated in terms of the individual point of view, 25, 77–80; yet the individual can define values truly only in terms of loyalty, 81–98; the true value of loyalty definable only through a theory of truth and reality, 301–312; the value of the world life, 392–398. See GOOD and LOYALTY.

VIRTUES: the commonplace as well as the fundamental virtues as special forms of loyalty to loyalty, 130. See also under LOYALTY.

WAR-SPIRIT: as an illustration of loyalty, 39–41, 53; in relation to Japanese Bushido, 72; is not usually just in its estimate of the enemy's loyalty, 109; is no more characteristic than many other forms of loyalty, 54, 102, 113; involves the evil of assailing the loyalty of the enemy, 115; how the war-spirit is to be judged in the light of the general principle of loyalty to loyalty, 214, 215.

WHITMAN, WALT: 98.

WILL: my duty as my own will brought to clear self-consciousness, 25; difficulty of defining what my own will is, 27–37; loyalty as a solution of the problem, 38–47. — The individual will, interest, and desire, determine the choice of the right cause, subject to the principle of loyalty to loyalty, 19, 39–42, 52–54, 58, 93, 110, 125, 130, 131, 138, 156, 157, 177, 186, 187, 226, cf. 117–128. — The "will of the world" in relation to our loyalty, 390–391; the individual will and the universal will, 395.

ZION: 279.

BOOKS ON PHILOSOPHY

A Student's History of Philosophy

By ARTHUR KENYON ROGERS, Professor of Philosophy in Butler College. First Edition, New York, 1901; Second Edition, 1907.

Cloth. 511 pages. 8vo. $2.00 net.

The book gives an account of philosophical development which includes all the material that can fairly be placed before the student beginning the study of the history of philosophy. The chief aim is to gain simplicity of statement without losing sight of the real meaning of philosophical problems. Wherever possible the author gives the thought of the writers in their own words, thus giving a literary interest and a hint at the personality behind the thought. This has been found a valuable device in interesting students in reading the masterpieces of philosophy at first hand. Although the author recognizes that the history of philosophy centres about the history of individual men, he has made his book distinctly a history of philosophy and not of philosophers.

The Persistent Problems of Philosophy

An Introduction to Philosophy through a Study of Modern Systems. By MARY WHITON CALKINS, Professor of Philosophy and Psychology at Wellesley College; Author of "An Introduction to Psychology," and "Der doppelte Standpunkt in der Psychologie." New York, 1907.

Cloth. 575 pages. 8vo. $2.50 net.

"It is exceptional in lucidity, candor, and the freshness with which it surveys well-worn doctrines. More than any Introduction to Philosophy with which I am acquainted, it will induce its reader to turn to the original sources, and to find pleasure in seeing Philosophy as it rises in the minds of the great thinkers. While the book is unusually attractive in style, and well fitted for popular use, it is the work of an original and critical scholar. The temper with which the history of philosophy should be studied finds here admirable expression." — Professor G. H. PALMER, *Department of Philosophy, Harvard University.*

A Brief Introduction to Modern Philosophy

By ARTHUR KENYON ROGERS, Professor of Philosophy in Butler College.

Cloth. 360 pages. 12mo. $1.25 net.

It shows, in as untechnical a way as possible, and with little presupposition of previous philosophical training, how the problems of philosophy arise out of any attempt to understand the world and to appreciate the value which belongs to human experience.

THE MACMILLAN COMPANY
PUBLISHERS, 64–66 FIFTH AVENUE, NEW YORK

A System of Metaphysics

By GEORGE STUART FULLERTON, Professor of Philosophy in Columbia University. New York, 1904.

Cloth. 627 pages. 8vo. $4.00 net.

An Introduction to Philosophy

By GEORGE STUART FULLERTON, Professor of Philosophy in Columbia University. New York, 1906.

Cloth. 322 pages. 12mo. $1.60 net.

A book for the thoughtful man who, tiring of the everlasting talk of things of practical value, turns aside from his work a little while to refresh himself with a review of some of those eternal questions which until the end of time must occupy the best minds of mankind.

The Problems of Philosophy

By HAROLD HÖFFDING. Translated by GALEN M. FISHER. New York, 1905.

Cloth. 201 pages. 16mo. $1.00 net.

"Professor Höffding, of Copenhagen, is one of the wisest, as well as one of the most learned, of living philosophers. . . . The following little work is, so to speak, his philosophical testament. In it he sums up in an extraordinarily compact and pithy form the result of his lifelong reflections on the deepest alternatives of philosophical opinions. The work, to my mind, is so pregnant and its conclusions so sensible — or at least so in accordance with what I regard as sensible — that I have had it translated as a contribution to the education of our English-reading students." — *Extract from preface by* Professor WILLIAM JAMES, *of Harvard University.*

Foundations of Knowledge

By ALEXANDER THOMAS ORMOND. London, 1900.

Cloth. 528 pages. 8vo. $3.00 net.

Concepts of Philosophy

By ALEXANDER THOMAS ORMOND, McCosh Professor of Philosophy in Princeton University. New York, 1906.

Cloth. 722 pages. 8vo. $4.00 net.

In Three Parts: Part I — Analysis; Part II — Syntax, (*a*) from Physics to Sociology; (*b*) from Sociology to Religion; Part III — Deductive.

The Limits of Evolution

And Other Essays illustrating the Metaphysical Theory of Personal Idealism. By G. H. HOWISON, LL.D., Mills Professor of Philosophy in the University of California. New York, First Edition, 1901; Second Edition, 1904.

Cloth. 450 pages. 12mo. $2.00 net.

THE MACMILLAN COMPANY
PUBLISHERS, 64-66 FIFTH AVENUE, NEW YORK

PSYCHOLOGY

An Outline of Psychology

By EDWARD BRADFORD TITCHENER, Sage Professor of Psychology in Cornell University. New York. First Edition, 1896; Second Edition, 1897; Third Edition, 1899.

Cloth, 370 pages. 12mo. $1.40 net.

A new edition of this important introductory text-book for college classes is to be issued in the near future.

A Primer of Psychology

By EDWARD BRADFORD TITCHENER, Sage Professor of Psychology in Cornell University. New York. First Edition, 1898; Second Edition, 1899.

Cloth. 316 pages. 12mo. $1.00 net.

Experimental Psychology

A Manual of Laboratory Practice. By EDWARD BRADFORD TITCHENER. In Four Volumes.

I. **Qualitative Experiments.** Part I — Student's Manual. New York, 1901. *Cloth. 214 pages. 8vo. $1.60 net.* Part II — Instructor's Manual. New York, 1901. *Cloth. 456 pages. 8vo. $2.50 net.*

II. **Quantitative Experiments.** Part I — Student's Manual. New York, 1905. *Cloth. 208 pages. $1.40 net.* Part II — Instructor's Manual. New York, 1905. *Cloth. 453 pages. 8vo. $2.50 net.*

Mental Development in the Child and Race

By JAMES MARK BALDWIN, Professor of Philosophy and Psychology in Johns Hopkins University.

Vol. I. Methods and Processes. Third Edition, New York, 1906.

Cloth. 477 pages. 8vo. $2.25 net.

Vol. II. Social and Ethical Interpretations. A Study in Social Psychology. Fourth Edition, New York, 1906.

Cloth. 606 pages. 8vo. $2.60 net.

An Introduction to Psychology

By MARY WHITON CALKINS, Professor of Philosophy and Psychology in Wellesley College. Second Edition, Revised, 1900.

Cloth. 512 pages. Crown 8vo. $2.00 net.

Outlines of Psychology

An Elementary Treatise with Some Practical Applications. By JOSIAH ROYCE, Professor of the History of Philosophy in Harvard University. New York, 1903.

Cloth. 392 pages. 12mo. $1.00 net.

THE MACMILLAN COMPANY
PUBLISHERS, 64–66 FIFTH AVENUE, NEW YORK

PHILOSOPHY OF RELIGION

"Nothing short of a complete revision of current theological ideas can bring permanent satisfaction to our highly reflective age." — JOHN WATSON.

The Philosophical Basis of Religion

A Series of Lectures by JOHN WATSON, M.A., LL.D., Professor of Moral Philosophy in Queen's University, Kingston, Canada.

Cloth. 485 pages. $3.00 net.

"Essays in the reconstruction and history of religious belief." — *Author's Preface.*

The Religious Conception of the World

By ARTHUR KENYON ROGERS, Professor of Philosophy and Education at Butler College. New York, 1907.

. Cloth. 285 pages. 12mo. $1.50 net.

An Introduction to the Philosophy of Religion

By JOHN CAIRD, Principal and Vice-Chancellor of the University of Glasgow. Glasgow, 1880.

Cloth. 343 pages. 12mo. $1.50 net.

The Philosophy of the Christian Religion

By ANDREW MARTIN FAIRBAIRN, Principal of Mansfield College, Oxford. New York, 1905.

Cloth. 583 pages. 8vo. $3.50 net.

The Psychological Elements of Religious Faith

Lectures by CHARLES CARROLL EVERETT, D.D., LL.D., Late Bussey Professor of Theology in Harvard University. Edited by EDWARD HALE, Professor of Homiletics in the Divinity School of Harvard University. New York, 1902.

Cloth. 215 pages. 12mo. $1.25 net.

The Psychology of Religious Belief

By JAMES BISSETT PRATT, Ph.D., Assistant Professor of Philosophy in Williams College. New York, 1907.

Cloth. 327 pages. 12mo. $1.50 net.

The Philosophy of Religion

By HAROLD HÖFFDING, Professor in the University of Copenhagen. Translated from the German edition, by P. E. MEYER. London, 1906.

410 pages. 8vo. $3.00 net.

THE MACMILLAN COMPANY
PUBLISHERS, 64–66 FIFTH AVENUE, NEW YORK

ImTheStory.com

Personalized Classic Books in many genre's

Unique gift for kids, partners, friends, colleagues

Customize:

- Character Names
- Upload your own front/back cover images (optional)
- Inscribe a personal message/dedication on the
  inside page (optional)

Customize many titles Including
- Alice in Wonderland
- Romeo and Juliet
- The Wizard of Oz
- A Christmas Carol
- Dracula
- Dr. Jekyll & Mr. Hyde
- And more...

Emily's Adventures In Wonderland

Ryan & Julia